CONVENIENT ACTION

Steve Howard
Chief Executive Officer

The Climate Group
The Tower Building
3rd Floor, York Road
London SE1 7NX
United Kingdom

FOREWORD

In December 2009, the world witnessed one of the biggest political gatherings for the cause of Climate Change in Copenhagen with participation of more than 190 nations from all over the world. One hundred and twenty heads of state attended – making it the largest gathering of leaders outside New York on any issue ever. Whilst the Copenhagen Accord did represent a step forward, it did not deliver on the high expectations of a legally binding international agreement. Add to it the fact that many developing countries have yet to meet their initial targets under the Kyoto Protocol and we realize that even when an international agreement is reached, it might take long before it is implemented in full spirit.

Meeting the challenge of Climate Change and delivering clean low carbon energy and prosperity will require the leadership of all levels of government. Scaling up the efforts requires the full engagement of sub national governments, whose decisions can influence 50% to 80% of the greenhouse gas emissions and most site-dependent adaptation initiatives. At The Climate Group, we strongly believe that the time has come to take up the discourse with sub national governments that have the power to make rapid transformations. Sub national governments are closer to the people than their national counterparts, can move more quickly and are closer to the results.

Gujarat is one State which is already getting on with implementing initiatives to transform itself into a low carbon economy and is making real changes. Building on a model of positive partnerships between people, businesses, scientific community and government, the State has shown real commitment. The fact that the Government has gone ahead and set up its own full fledged department of Climate Change, is a clear declaration of intent and shows that the actions have been well-planned and thought through. Demonstrated models like these are required all over the world which will help advance practical policy development on the issue of Climate Change. I would call this unique compendium of action a 'Green Autobiography' of Narendra Modi who has shown a definite path and determined strategy to meet the Challenges of Climate Change, as we approach Cancun for COP16.

Steve Howard

" In whom the sea, canals, lakes, wells, tanks, in whom our food and cornfields had their being, in whom this all that breathes and moves is active may this Earth (bhumi) grant us all excellent eatable and drinkable objects like milk, fruits, water and cereals. "

Atharva Veda (A.V.) 12.1.3

यस्यां समुद्र उत सिन्धुरापो यस्यामन्नं कृष्टयः सम्बभूवुः ।
यस्यामिदं जिन्वति प्राणदेजत्सा नो भूमिः पूर्वपेये दधातु ॥ ३ ॥

River Sabarmati, Western India

"... the purity in us is due to the Earth. The Earth is my mother and I (the seer) am Her son. Cloud is my Father, let that nourish us."

Atharva Veda (A.V.) 12.1.12

यत्ते मध्यं पृथिवि यच्च नभ्यं यास्त ऊर्जस्तन्वः सम्बभूवुः ।
तासु नो धेह्यभि नः पवस्व माता भूमिः पुत्रो अहं पृथिव्याः ॥
पर्जन्यः पिता स उ नः पिपर्तु ॥ १२ ॥

Nature as God

"- and naturally the beauties and sublimities of nature captivate the attention of man first. The first questions that arose in the human soul were about the external world. The solution of the mystery was asked of the sky, of the stars, of the heavenly bodies, of the earth, of the rivers, of the mountains, of the ocean, and in all ancient religions we find traces of how the groping human mind at first caught at everything external. There was a river-god, a sky-god, a cloud-god, a rain-god; everything external, all of which we now call the powers of nature, became metamorphosed, transfigured, into wills, into gods, into heavenly messengers."

THE COSMOS The Microcosm
(Delivered in New York, 26th January, 1896), Complete Works of **Swami Vivekanand,** Volume 2.

Vivekanand Memorial Kanyakumari

"One must care about a world one will not see."

Mahatma Gandhi
(1869-1948)

© *Narendra Modi, Gandhinagar, Gujarat, 2011*

All rights reserved. No part of this publication may be reproduced or transmitted, in any form or by any means, without permission. Any person who does any unauthorised act in relation to this publication may be liable to criminal prosecution and civil claims for damages.

First published, 2011

MACMILLAN PUBLISHERS INDIA LTD
Delhi Bangalore Chennai Kolkata Mumbai
Ahmedabad Bhopal Chandigarh Coimbatore Cuttack
Guwahati Hubli Hyderabad Jaipur Lucknow Madurai
Nagpur Patna Pune Thiruvananthapuram Visakhapatnam

Companies and representatives throughout the world

ISBN 10: 0230-331920
ISBN 13: 978-0230-331921

Published by Rajiv Beri for Macmillan Publishers India Ltd
2/10 Ansari Road, Daryaganj, New Delhi 110 002

Printed in India.

CONVENIENT ACTION
Gujarat's Response To Challenges Of Climate Change

NARENDRA MODI

Grateful

The earth is lovely
These eyes are grateful.

    Here the sunlight pours onto lush green grass
        Sunlight cannot be captured though.

The sky is gorgeous
And the earth is lovely.

        The rainbow blossoming in the sky
        Drawing circles of colour in the air.

Of which past birth these good deeds are?
Life is grateful, grateful.

        The sea rocks up towards the sky.
        Who knows what lies in the womb of clouds!

This nothingness is meaningful
The earth is lovely.

        I have mingled with fair of human beings
        And recognised myself in the company of others.

All this is unique
And something is mystical.

        Grateful grateful grateful it is
        My earth is lovely.

Narendra Modi

Source: *Aankh Aa Dhanya Chhe*, 2007

Introduction

With my humble moorings in a small village ensconced in rural hinterland of Western India, I grew up in an atmosphere that was more in harmony with nature than the inhospitable, polluted and haphazard landscapes of big cities where I shifted in due course. Respect for nature was inextricably embedded in our culture at home, so much so that we were told by my mother to fold hands and ask for Mother Earth's forgiveness after getting up in the morning before putting our feet down on ground. This, I realised a few years later in life, was the social integration of the philosophy of Vedas in India. Vedas have been the oldest repertoire of ancient knowledge. They have laid the foundation of Hindu religion and have provided an enlightened path of development of Hindu culture and lifestyle.

My views on complementary relationship between man and nature took definite shape when I studied the *Prithvi-Sukta* of *Atharva Veda* during my college days. The sixty-three Suktas, (couplets) composed thousands of years ago, contain a whole spectrum of knowledge which is now being propounded under various scientific, academic and analytical banners during discussions on global warming, damage to earth's environment and the resultant Climate Change. The underlying spirit is that of a mother-son relationship between man and earth; and the rain clouds that fill the earth with life sustaining water have been likened to the father. The bounties of nature in circulating waters of streams, seas and oceans, hills, snowy mountains and forests, all have to be guarded and replenished if used, so as to yield us a sustainable amount of food, milk and other agricultural products and ultimately bestow us with splendour, strength and brilliance. Sustainability is ultimately a moral issue since it involves the protection of interests of our future generations. Climate Change is definitely affecting the future generations which, as of now, have no voice on the actions of present generation. A UN report has termed this as 'unsustainable ecological debt' which our generation is running up for the future generations to inherit. The two Suktas of *Atharva Veda* had embodied the very same message thousands of years ago:

> "We aspire to live long, our children too would live long and be free from sickness and consumption. We all are reared up in the lap of the Mother Earth. May we have long life (provided) we are watchful and alert and sacrifice our all for Her."
>
> *Atharva Veda* (A.V.) 12.1.62

> "With an utter sense of ethics and dutiful attitude, we can live happily in an honourable position. It is reiterated that the revolving Earth, of one accord with the Sun sets the supersentient seer in glory and in wealth."
>
> *Atharva Veda* (A.V.) 12.1.63

Rig Veda has also emphasised on the importance of Panch Tatvas (five elements) namely Prithvi (earth), Pavan (air), Jal (water), Tej (solar energy) and Nabh (sky) and has maintained that the entire life systems on earth are based on harmonious functioning of these five elements. Therefore, sustainable use of these natural elements has been consistently advocated in all ancient Indian scriptures like the *Rig Veda, Manu Smriti, Yagyavalkya Smriti*, etc. It has, time and again, been emphasised in these scriptures that man should use these heavenly gifts in such a way that no long term damage is caused to them. The energies and benefits derived proportionately from these five elements will only sustain life and preserve mother earth. Any disproportionate exploitation of these energies will cause pollution and will promote selfishness, instincts of violence, jealousy – inimical to human development. And this is precisely what has happened during the last hundred years and has disturbed the natural equilibrium.

My views on this issue were further inspired by Mahatma Gandhi's concept of Trusteeship which was basically propounded in the colonial context. This concept exhorted the rich to use their wealth only for fulfilling the right to an honourable livelihood no better than that enjoyed by millions of others. The rest of the wealth should belong to the community and must be used for the welfare of the community. To apply the concept of trusteeship in the context of Climate Change, I firmly believe that our present generation should act as trustees for the wealth of nature and should use it only in a sustainable way so that it can also be enjoyed by many generations to come. Mahatma Gandhi was absolutely right when he said that everything belonged to God and was from God and hence no individual is entitled to more than his proportionate portion and, therefore, he became a trustee of the rest of proportion for God's people. Unfortunately, the reckless destruction of ecological harmony has heightened the responsibility of our generation and specially those living in the developed world to act as trustees in the real sense of the term for future generations. Therefore, ethics and equity in my view are at the core of debate on Climate Change.

I remember, a few years ago, I used to read a lot of sceptic views on Climate Change, whether or not it was actually happening. Having been in public life I am aware of behind-the-scene lobbying by vested interests that normally accompany any such carefully orchestrated campaigns. But even in those days of uncertainty and confusion, I based the formulation of public policy on my conviction of complementary relationship between man and nature. This helped me to clarify my thoughts and to choose a developmental path that would lead to empowerment of the poor and downtrodden in a way that would make the sustainable use of the bounties of nature. It was only after following consistently, for almost eight years, the developmental philosophy as Chief Minister of a State (with around 196,000 km^2 area and around 55 million inhabitants) that I decided to document these successful experimentations.

This book, therefore, is only a humble attempt to document, initiatives and innovations that we have undertaken and experimented during the last eight years in Gujarat, that have directly or indirectly but significantly contributed and will continue to contribute to the adaptation and mitigation of Climate Change. It should, in no way, be looked upon as a stereotype, or a governmental propaganda to highlight a political leader's achievements. Having been an ardent follower, for about five decades, of a nationalistic ideology based on strong foundations of sacrifice, selfless service and cultural conviction, I have been inspired to do and follow what is morally correct and beneficial to mankind at large. Therefore, this book apart from documenting our multidimensional initiative, is also an open and polite invitation to the world community of scholars, researchers, scientists, leaders and policy planners to visit my State of Gujarat, experience and feel the impact, and measure and judge them against any yardsticks of scientific and analytical scrutiny.

Dichotomy between dominant interventionist model of development and decentralised participative model had been in my mind when I started my development journey in Gujarat eight years ago. I have attempted to turn this conflict into cooperation by a synthesis of both strategies in my model of Gujarat development. There were many areas and sectors where I realised that stand-alone initiatives by Government would neither address the problems effectively nor would result in sustainability or even create a sense of belonging. In particular, dealing with water scarcity in parched lands of Saurashtra region (south western Gujarat) by creating a sustainable network of micro irrigation and recharge structures; was a challenge that could only be handled by mass participation supplemented by financial and technical support provided by Government. In this case, I could synthesise two development approaches mentioned earlier. Resultantly, a solution was found to drinking water and irrigation needs of millions of people, recharge of depleted ground water resources and revival of surrounding ecology by hundreds of oasis in those dry regions of Gujarat. In retrospect, within a Climate Change paradigm, this has definitely improved water availability and quality, increased soil fertility and thereby agricultural productivity (from a single rain-fed crop a year to three crops per annum in many cases) and led to betterment in air quality by arresting the trend of desertification of lands in these areas. To put into proper perspective, what I am referring to here is an area covering around 142,700 km^2 with 27.63 million inhabitants. This initiative of development of community based infrastructure for water harvesting has reduced vulnerability and empowered people to cope with Climate Change impacts in my State and has come in for a special mention in UNDP Human Development Report 2007-2008.

But replacing the use of gasoline by a more environment friendly alternative – Compressed Natural Gas (CNG) in large number of vehicles in Gujarat required direct intervention from the Government in order to create an infrastructure of supply and distribution. In just a span of two years, we converted more than three hundred thousand vehicles into CNG and achieved remarkable results in improving ambient air quality in the city of Ahmedabad with four million inhabitants. This has been an initiative with definite Climate Change mitigation overtones. Similarly, turning the largely Government dominated State capital Gandhinagar into a solar city by captive solar and wind energy production for Government usage, again required direct intervention. Hence, this queer admixture of two development strategies, otherwise thought by many to be mutually exclusive, has enabled me to accomplish several initiatives with Climate Change adaptation and mitigation potential.

UN Secretary General Ban Ki Moon got a very strong case of action prepared and published in Human Development Report, 2007, for fighting Climate Change. A very timely plea indeed for governments, institutions and stakeholders world over. My attempt to prepare this compendium of action taken, thus far, is only an extension of that plea in order to inspire all those concerned, that within a democratic framework and despite electoral constraints things can and will happen if they are planned and executed with single-minded devotion to a larger cause and with a firm determination to fight Climate Change.

Al Gore was right when he commented a few years ago that it was inconvenient to many leaders to hear, face and accept the naked truth of Global Warming. I would go further by saying that the real test of leadership is not only in welcoming this truth but also in devising, formulating and implementing a strategy that results in what I call decisive, appropriate, timely and 'convenient action' to deal with this truth and the challenges that it has thrown.

from water riots to water security

Before the year 2001 drinking water scarcity had posed serious threat to human and cattle lives in Gujarat State. Successively, Governments had to spend billions of rupees on temporary measures to supply drinking water by road tankers and some times even through special water trains. The State, which generally had a track record of peace and cooperative social ethos, even witnessed 'water riots' due to severe water scarcity compounded by poor water resources management.

Water Riots In Gujarat

Police preventing a self-immolation bid by two activists of Sankalp Seva Samiti at the east zone office compound of Ahmedabad Municipal Corporation in Rakhiyal area over water supply problem
Newsline Photo

From Water Riots To Water Security

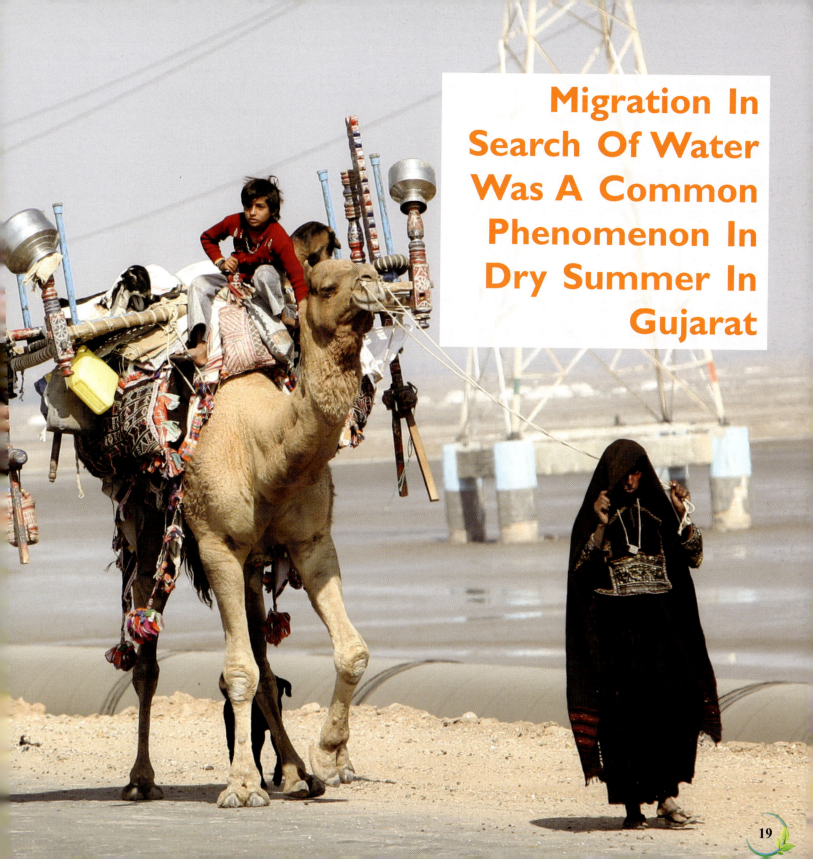
Migration In Search Of Water Was A Common Phenomenon In Dry Summer In Gujarat

From Water Riots To Water Security

Daily Drudgery Of Women

Lack of access to safe drinking water, time loss in collecting available water, effects of head loading and the burden of household responsibilities – all cause detrimental effects on the health of women and general family welfare including their income-earning abilities.

Plight Of The People In Rural Areas
District Surendranagar, Gujarat

From Water Riots To Water Security

Women Struggle For Water In Rural Areas

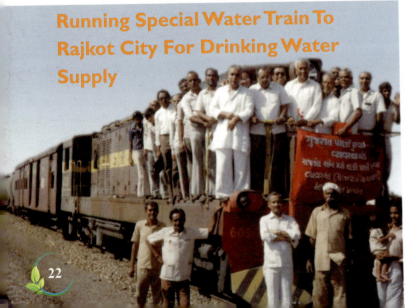

Running Special Water Train To Rajkot City For Drinking Water Supply

Transportation Of Drinking Water To Rajula Through Railway Wagons

Long Queues For Water - Detrimental To Health And Family Welfare

From Water Riots To Water Security

Transporting Water Through Road Tankers

Over drafting of ground water (as compared to annual recharge) caused serious water quality problems due to excessive fluoride, nitrate and salinity. The number of fluoride affected habitations increased from 2,826 in the year 1992 to 4,187 by the year 2003. The fluoride concentration in these villages ranged from 1.5 mg/litre to as high as 18.90 mg/litre. Fluoride has been the cause of extensive health damages in many parts of Gujarat. Dental fluorosis causes permanent pigmentation of teeth in children and bone deformities are caused by skeletal fluorosis even in adults. Other serious problems experienced due to high concentration of fluoride have been aneamia, loss of appetite, nausea and thyroid malfunction which sometimes results in brain impairment of children and adverse impact on foetus, in some cases causing abortion or stillbirth in expectant mothers.

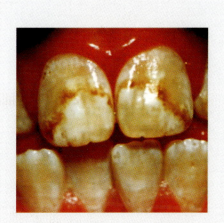
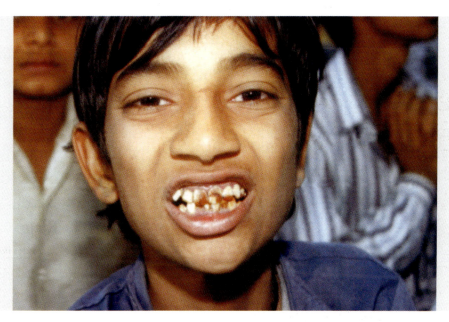

Future Generation Permanently Deformed By Dental Fluorosis

From Water Riots To Water Security

After taking over the reins of Gujarat, dealing with water stress and water insecurity was a big challenge for me. We drew up an ambitious strategy for creating a 'State Wide Drinking Water Grid' for bulk water transmission from sustainable surface water resources to water scarce and poor water quality habitations.

Large scale infrastructure has been created for this purpose, which includes 1,987 km of bulk pipelines and more than 115,058 km of distribution pipelines. About 10,781 hydraulic structures like elevated storage reservoirs with a total capacity of 1,164 million litres and 10,683 storage sumps and high ground level reservoirs with a capacity of 2,504.80 million litres have also been constructed in the State. Along with this, 151 water filtration and treatment plants having a total capacity of 2,750 million litres per day (MLD) have been constructed. About 2,250 MLD of treated water is delivered to more than 10,501 villages and 127 towns in the State for ensuring safe and assured water supply to about 65% of State's population in drought prone and water quality affected areas through the water supply grid.

All these efforts have resulted into considerable relief from the problem of excessive fluoride contamination. As per a recent survey, only 987 habitations have been found to be affected and the range of fluoride content has also shrunk considerably.

Permanent Disability By Skeletal Fluorosis

From Water Riots To Water Security

Prior to the implementation of the ambitious master plan for drought proofing, most of the drinking water supply was based on ground water for which deep tubewells with high capacity pumping machinery were being utilised in the State.

Water Treatment Plant And Elevated Storage Reservoir
Dharoi, District Mehsana, Gujarat

From Water Riots To Water Security

Pumping Stations For Drinking Water Supply

Dharoi, District Mehsana, Gujarat

Mahi Pariej, District Kheda, Gujarat

The tubewells in north Gujarat and Saurashtra regions in the State were tapping deeper and deeper aquifers for which electricity consumption was very high. Therefore, a 'vicious circle' was operating in relation to water and energy with considerable environmental and health costs.

The surface based water supply through pipelines being operated by centralised hydraulic structures has resulted in significant reduction of use of tubewells in these regions for drinking water supply. The number of such tubewells from 1985-86 to 2007-08 every year is shown in following figure.

Number Of Tubewells Installed

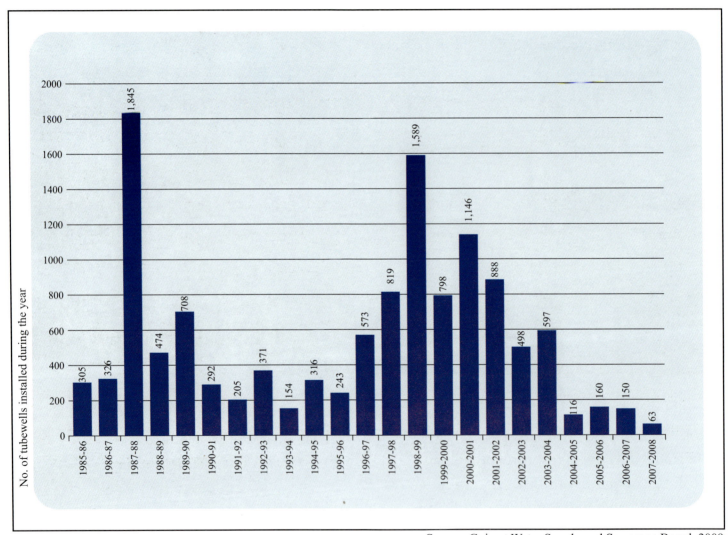

Source: Gujarat Water Supply and Sewerage Board, 2009

This has also resulted in sharp decline in expenditure on tanker water supply in the State from 2003-04 onwards, which is another indicator of creation of water security in the State.

Annual Expenditure On Tanker Supply From 1990 To 2009

Year	Villages	Cost (₹ in Million)*	Year	Villages	Cost (₹ in Million)*
1990-91	896	23.40	2001-2002	2,959	348.11
1991-92	1,943	92.90	2002-2003	3,961	475.36
1992-93	700	14.00	Sub-Total		2,168.06
1993-94	1,803	83.00	2003-2004	600	47.38
1994-95	724	24.96	2004-2005	869	92.32
1995-96	1,619	96.03	2005-2006	398	77.06
1996-97	1,642	123.95	2006-2007	207	17.08
1997-98	1,447	62.19	2007-2008	188	14.17
1998-99	1,215	41.02	2008-2009	326	13.94
1999-2000	2,987	346.20	Sub-Total		261.95
2000-2001	4,054	436.94	Total		2,430.01

*1 US$ ≅ ₹ 47

Source: Gujarat Water Supply and Sewerage Board, 2009

Decentralised Community Managed Water Supply Programme
Water And Sanitation Management Organisation (WASMO)

The creation of Water and Sanitation Management Organisation (WASMO) was a paradigm shift in the role of governance from provider to facilitator by empowering village level institutions through extensive capacity building and pro-active facilitation. Since its inception, WASMO has been able to bring in effective citizens' engagement through its innovative governance model for facilitating the successful community led water supply programme throughout the State of Gujarat. Now more than 16,740 Village Water and Sanitation Committees have been formed in the State that are ready to take the responsibility of management of service delivery and water resources management at the decentralised level. More than 6,500 villages have already commissioned the infrastructure and water conservation projects in a demand driven mode. Another 4,547 villages are presently implementing the decentralised community managed rural water supply programme in their villages with a strong feeling of ownership.

WASMO's strength lies in its organisational professionalism, innovations in governance, and strong partnerships with about 48 civil society organisations. The rural community is the central focus of WASMO's decentralised approach. Its innovation has led to the scaling up of reform processes to cover the entire State. Its professionals have created an enabling environment, which has resulted in, the community being fully empowered to take ownership of their water service delivery wherein operation and maintenance is done through tariff mechanism devised by consensus in the village assembly. It has also been able to institutionalise the rural water quality monitoring and surveillance programme. Majority of villages are now able to monitor their water quality through field test kits provided to a group of 5 to 6 persons of village water quality team which is duly trained. WASMO was given Prime Minister's award for Excellence in Public Administration for the year 2006-07. WASMO's innovation by my Government has emerged as a model for learning and exchange, influencing policy initiatives in the water sector at the country level. WASMO has also been given the United Nations Public Service Award in the category of fostering participation in policy-making decisions through innovative mechanisms.

WASMO's Outreach At A Glance
Decentralised Community Managed Water Supply Programme

No. of Village Water and Sanitation Committees (VWSCs) formed	16,740 (92% of total villages)
No. of projects commissioned by VWSCs	6,500
No. of projects under implementation	4,547
No. of villages having institutionalised tariff mechanisms	4,553
Total fund allocated to villages	₹ 10,782.80 Million*
Community contribution towards capital cost received from villages	₹ 1,078.20 Million*
No. of women headed VWSCs	2,800
Total number of women in VWSCs	49,986
No. of NGOs as partner Implementation Support Agencies (ISAs)	48
No. of districts covered	All 26 districts

User Level Water Quality Monitoring and Surveillance

Villages where awareness generation campaigns are taken up	All 18,600 villages
Villages where water quality teams are formed	14,804
Water quality kits distribution to villages	14,216
Water quality kits distribution to Municipalities	159
No. of persons trained for Water Quality Monitoring and Surveillance	1,54,591
No. of bacteriological testing vials distributed	11,72,500
No. of villages from where Water Quality Surveillance results are retrieved from local teams	18,600
Sanitary surveys conducted	40,142
Mapping of drinking water sources	32,923
Multi-districts assessment of water safety done with the help of UNICEF	14 districts

Source: Narmada, Water Resources, Water Supply and Kalpasar Department, 2009

*1 US$ ≅ ₹ 47

In several villages, the borewells are now utilised as a dual source and the operational hours have been reduced. Based on a random survey, it has been observed that a significant saving has been achieved in electricity consumption that is now available for alternative uses proving to be an eco-friendly achievement. Solar pumps have also been commissioned in 260 villages in the State and about 200 more solar pumping systems will be installed in the near future. In various parts of the State, including coastal and tribal areas, roof top rain water harvesting structures have also been taken up in public buildings, schools and individual household level, which is also resulting in substantial electricity savings. Comprehensive energy audits for various group water supply schemes have also resulted in energy savings.

It is estimated that approximately 72.09 million kWh of electricity is being conserved per annum due to operationalisation of surface based water supply through the pipelines in the State. The above mentioned measures have resulted in saving of about 16,076 tCO_2 equivalent emissions per annum, conservatively calculated.

Narmada Based Water Supply
Nabhoi, District Gandhinagar, Gujarat

Emission Savings In Drinking Water Supply

Sr. No.	Particulars	Energy Saving MWh per Annum	Equivalent Carbon Dioxide Emission per annum in tonnes
1.	Piped water supply to villages and towns	65,905.00	14,696.82
2.	Savings due to energy audit	5,184.78	1,156.21
3.	Solar based pumping systems	611.16	136.29
4.	Rooftop rain water harvesting	386.74	86.24
	Total	72,087.68	16,076.14

Source: Gujarat Water Supply and Sewerage Board, 2009

With a paradigm shift from dependence on drinking water supply by tankers, trains and deep bore wells to safe surface water, much of the fluoride affected habitations have been covered by piped water supply.

Technological interventions like defluoridation through reverse osmosis have also been taken up in some villages. In the remaining villages safe water sources have been identified or created and are being used for drinking water purpose. Thus, a 'vicious circle' has been transformed into a 'virtuous cycle' with a win-win situation for water, energy, environment and health sectors and with considerable economic benefits. In short, this is our action oriented response to the existing and future water stress and insecurity due to Climate Change.

Status Of Fluoride Affected Habitations

District	No. of Total Habitations	As per 2003 survey	As per recent survey	Maximum Fluoride level (PPM)
Ahmedabad	727	120	20	7.20
Gandhinagar	424	132	2	6.27
Patan	651	246	43	13.25
Mehsana	851	176	2	4.40
Sabarkantha	2,438	531	9	6.93
Banaskantha	1,736	521	20	5.75
Surendranagar	696	205	72	8.72
Rajkot	871	126	120	5.40
Jamnagar	756	52	5	2.00
Junagadh	925	76	48	2.80
Porbandar	184	46	0	3.70
Bhavnagar	804	108	66	6.40
Amreli	650	49	146	3.20
Kutch	1,126	34	6	3.20
Vadodara	2,187	438	189	5.81
Narmada	722	49	0	2.60
Kheda	2,101	406	52	10.03
Anand	920	96	17	5.89
Panchmahals	2,531	401	86	6.40
Dahod	3,168	286	0	12.50
Surat	3,258	44	29	2.20
Bharuch	790	21	30	4.00
Valsad	3,923	2	25	1.79
Navsari	2,080	22	0	--
Dangs	326	0	0	--
Total	**34,845**	**4,187**	**987**	

Source: Gujarat Water Supply and Sewerage Board, 2009

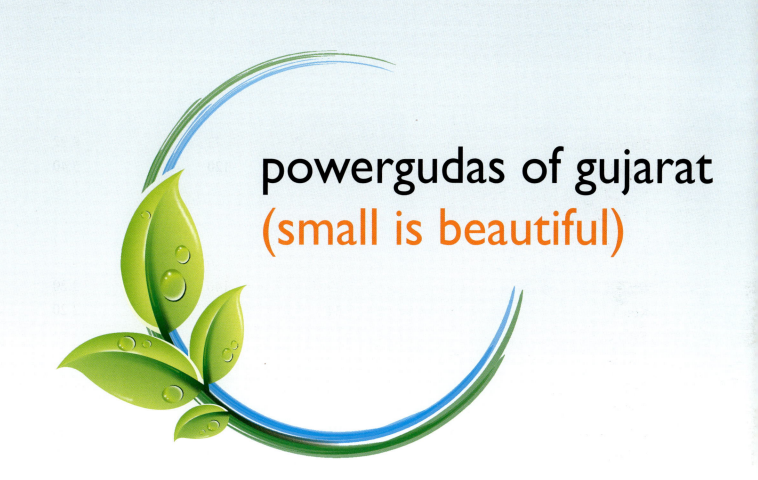

Powergudas Of Gujarat (Small Is Beautiful)

In 2004, a small village known as 'Powerguda' in the southern Indian State of Andhra Pradesh shot to fame by selling carbon credits worth ₹ 32,000* (equivalent to having saved 147 tCO_2) by replacing diesel used in water pumping engines by bio fuel produced from *Pongamia Pinnata,* a native tree species found in the local forest.

*1 US$ ≅ ₹ 47

Water Harvesting Structure
District Bhavnagar, Gujarat

Year	Expenditure	Storage Capacity
2005-06	₹ 193,000*	8,450 m³

Powergudas Of Gujarat (Small Is Beautiful)

Water Harvesting Structure
District Junagadh, Gujarat

World Bank bought those Carbon Credits to neutralise the emissions from air travel and local transport of World Bank officials. A good practice indeed! But let me confess, I had no Powerguda in mind while exhorting my officials to join hands with people in parched lands of different parts of Gujarat in 2004 in order to create checkdams and village ponds. My sole motivation was to reduce the miseries of

*1 US$ ≅ ₹ 47

millions of small and marginal farmers due to the vagaries of nature and difficult terrains through rainwater harvesting by micro irrigation structures.

Checkdams were designed to cope with the flow of water from rivulets and streams with a maximum height of 1.5 to 2.0 m with the storage varying from 0.015 MCM to 0.035 MCM.

Year	Expenditure	Storage Capacity
2004-05	₹ 128,000*	4,650 m³

Farm Pond
District Valsad, Gujarat

The Sardar Patel Participatory Water Conservation Project (SPPWCP) stipulated that checkdams, village tanks/ponds could be taken up for construction by a beneficiary group or any Non-Governmental Organization (NGO) with technical and financial assistance from the District Panchayat (local representative body). They were initially required to contribute 40% of the estimated costs (later reduced to 10%) and the rest was to be funded by the Government depending upon the progress of the work. In 2007 they were also given the option of contributing their 10% share by way of physical labour and, therefore, increasing their sense of belonging to the project by 'the gospel of dirty hands'. Six prototype designs were circulated with a maximum cost of ₹ 1,000,000*.

Powergudas Of Gujarat (Small Is Beautiful)

Year: 2008-09
Expenditure: ₹115,000*
Water Storage: 5,200 m³

*1 US$ ≅ ₹ 47

Farm Pond
District Kutch, Gujarat

Details Of Standard Farm Pond Size

Sr. No.	Farm Pond Overall Area in m²	Size of Farm Ponds (in m)			Storage Capacity in m³	Average Expenditure ₹*
		Top	Bottom	Depth		
1.	324 (18x18)	18	14	3	776	23,280
2.	400 (20x20)	20	16	3	980	29,400
3.	529 (23x23)	23	19	3	1,331	39,930
4.	625 (25x25)	25	21	3	1,595	47,850
5.	900 (30x30)	30	22	3	2,060	60,600
6.	1600 (40x40)	40	32	3	3,920	117,600

Source: Gujarat Land Development Corporation, 2009

Powergudas Of Gujarat (Small Is Beautiful)

Village Pond
District Ahmedabad, Gujarat

Year: 2007-08
Expenditure: ₹ 497,000*
Water Storage: 20,800 m³

*1 US$ ≅ ₹ 47

Details Of Standard Village Pond Size

Sr. No.	Village Pond Overall Area in m²	Size of Village Ponds (in m)			Storage Capacity in m³	Average Expenditure ₹*
		Top	Bottom	Depth		
1.	3,600 (60x60)	60	56	2	6,736	202,080
2.	5,625 (75x75)	75	71	2	10,666	319,980
3.	10,000 (100x100)	100	96	2	19,216	576,480

Source: Gujarat Land Development Corporation, 2009

> — the localised rainwater harvesting systems in the form of checkdams contain a proven solution to water crisis by recharging priceless groundwater resources of Saurashtra installing a decentralised drought proofing system and involving people in critical water management tasks, with simple, local skill based, cost effective and environment friendly technologies.

Source : Centre for Management in Agriculture, Indian Institute of Management, Ahmedabad, India

However, the beneficiary groups were also given the latitude to take up the work as per their own design, if necessary and feasible. The technical scrutiny and work supervision would be done by the engineers of the local body. The entire responsibility of the quality of construction of work, however, would rest with the beneficiary group/NGO under continuous guidance and technical inputs from the Government technical staff. Maintenance works for these micro water harvesting structures would be carried out by the beneficiary group at their own expense.

A total of 353,937 checkdams and village ponds/tanks have been created in the last eight years providing direct benefit to over 13 million people in rural Gujarat.

The average depletion of water levels in north Gujarat before the launch of this massive programme was around 3 m per year, which by now, would have cumulatively declined by almost 20-25 m – leading to sharp rise in electric consumption for drawl of ground water. But there has been a reported average water level rise of about 4 m during recent years as shown in the chart.

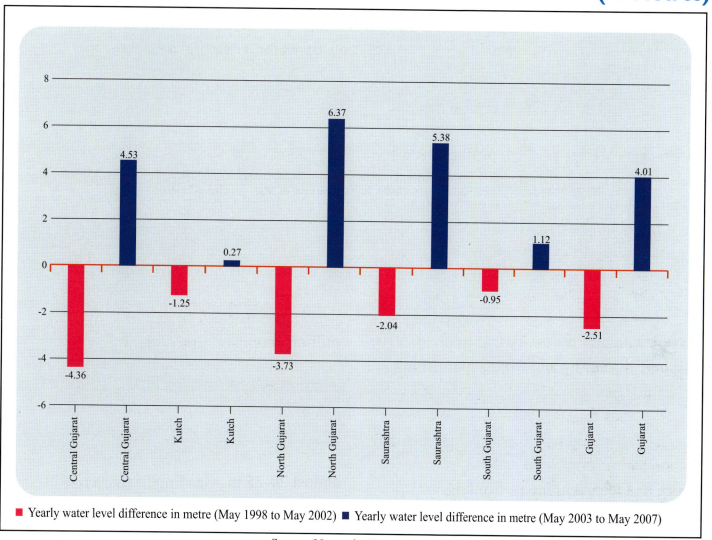

Source: Narmada, Water Resources, Water Supply and Kalpasar Department, 2009

Powergudas Of Gujarat (Small Is Beautiful)

On a macro level, irrigation efficiency has been improved and transmission and evaporation losses reduced. Around 357,000 ha of land has been covered under Participatory Irrigation Management leading to yield increase and water, fertiliser, labour and energy savings. It has been estimated that around 74.1 million kWh energy has been saved in just one year due to the adoption of drip irrigation by Gujarat Green Revolution Company – a body specially created for the purpose. Myriads of micro water harvesting structures dotting the landscape of Gujarat have led to the reduction in soil moisture evaporation in the surrounding agricultural fields and have facilitated the creation of orchards in places which barely used to produce single rain fed crops. Employment opportunities have been created for local residents, agricultural production has been enhanced, leading to rise in household incomes. The living standards and the average productivity of milch cattle has also gone up due to year-around availability of fodder. When I look back, I feel happy that we have created hundreds of thousands of Powergudas in Gujarat. If one Powerguda could save 147 tCO_2 emission, the cumulative achievement of these checkdams, farm and village tanks and ponds, etc., would definitely be millions of tCO_2 emission saving.

Public Participation in Micro Water Harvesting
North Gujarat

Water Temples

During my various interactions with small and marginal farmers in the State, I have been using socio-religious analogies for inculcating upon them the culture of water conservation. Social ethos in rural areas is more prone to be pro-actively driven for a particular cause by invoking religious beliefs and, therefore, I have been encouraging these farmers to make 'Water Temples' by digging farm ponds and village ponds. This religious similie of equating water ponds with temples has lent religious reverence for the preservation and conservation of water through these ponds. I have also been telling farmers that however poor household theirs may be, they must be keeping an earthen pot full of water for drinking purpose. Similarly village and farm ponds are like water pots for mother earth for quenching her thirst. And farmers are duty bound to create them as an obligation towards mother earth. This has further enhanced, through belief system, the creation of micro water harvesting structures in different parts of Gujarat.

Agriculture And Climate Change

Apart from creating hundreds of thousands of micro irrigation structures, we have adopted a consistent strategy to cope with Climate Changes in different agro-climatic zones of Gujarat:

- In each agro-climatic zone, there is one Agro-meteorological field unit, which provides weather based agro-advisory services to the farmers of that zone. This has helped the farmers to adopt better management practices and also to take preventive measures against any adverse effects of weather.

- Agro-climate based crop planning initiated through the Soil Health Card programme of my Government, in which

Agro Meteorological Unit
District Navsari, Gujarat

a cropping system has been suggested based on soil moisture availability index and has helped farmers to adopt better remunerative crops, thereby increasing their incomes.

- Agriculture Universities have initiated steps to create a network of observatories in Gujarat by installing automatic weather stations at different research locations in order to generate online weather information and to create a data bank on climate.

- Researches on the effects of Climate Change have been initiated on breeding of heat and photoperiod insensitive crop varieties and erection of poly houses to create controlled environment. This has increased the yield and reduced population dynamics of insects, pests and diseases, etc.

- We have established "Centre for Weather Forecasting and Climate Change" at Anand, "Centre for Environmental Studies" at Navsari and "Centre for Agro-advisory Services" at Junagadh. These centres are engaged in critical analysis of weather/climate parameters and their likely impacts on agricultural production.

- In addition to these, at Anand centre, two projects have been initiated in collaboration with SAC, ISRO, Ahmedabad and IIT Delhi, under which 40 Agricultural Weather Station (AWS) will be installed in Gujarat. These will provide better weather forecast at extended range or at seasonal scale and will be beneficial for climate risk management.

The cumulative effect of all this has been an increase in productivity of the major crops of the State, despite 0.1°C to 0.9°C average increase in temperatures recorded at various locations during the last couple of years. As compared to other States in India, Gujarat is an outstanding performer in agriculture, growing at the rate of 9.6% per annum. Though there is high volatility in agricultural growth rates for almost all States in India, performance of Gujarat's agriculture is more than thrice the all India figure. International Food Policy Research Institute, in a year 2009 document, has specially commended Gujarat's recent growth in cotton, fruits and vegetables and wheat production.

Increase In Productivity Of Crops In Gujarat (Average of Triennium)

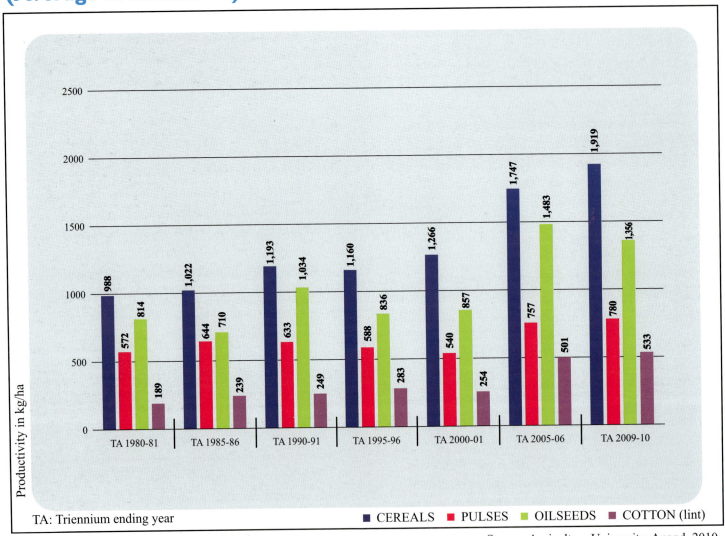

TA: Triennium ending year

Source: Agriculture University, Anand, 2010

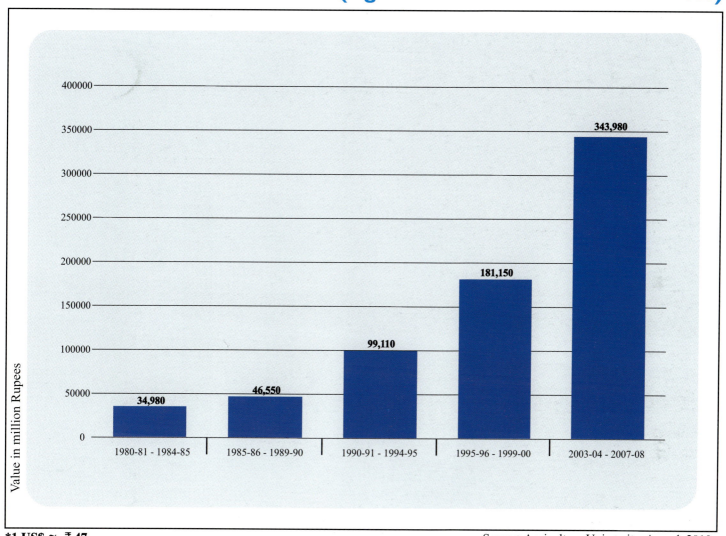

Increase In Productivity Of Rice In Gujarat

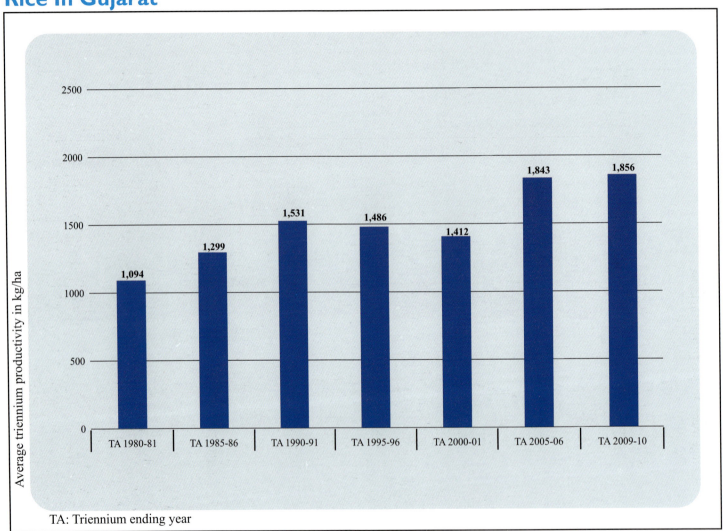

Source: Agriculture University, Navsari, 2010

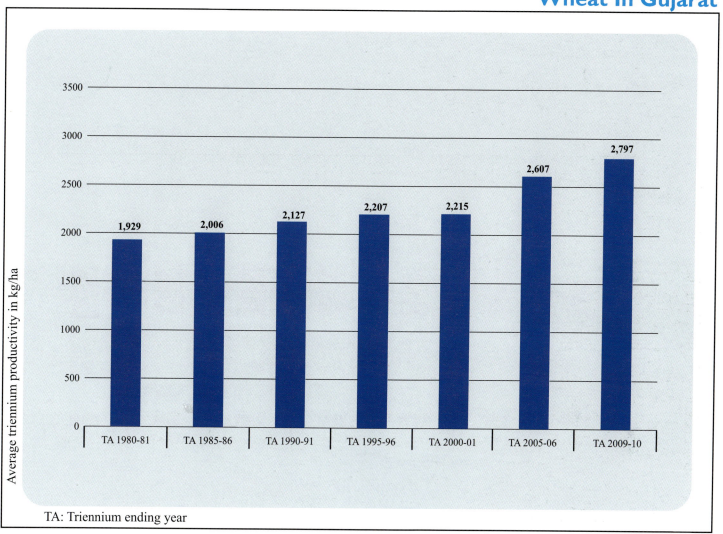

Increase In Productivity Of Groundnut In Gujarat

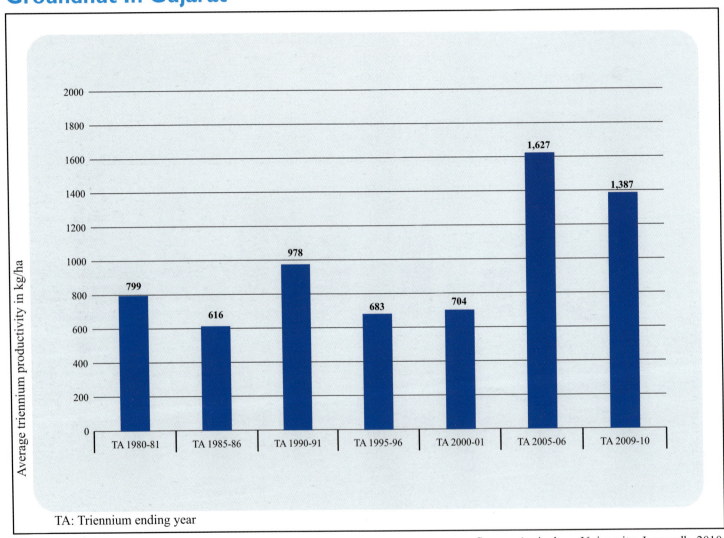

Source: Agriculture University, Junagadh, 2010

Increase In Productivity Of Castor In Gujarat

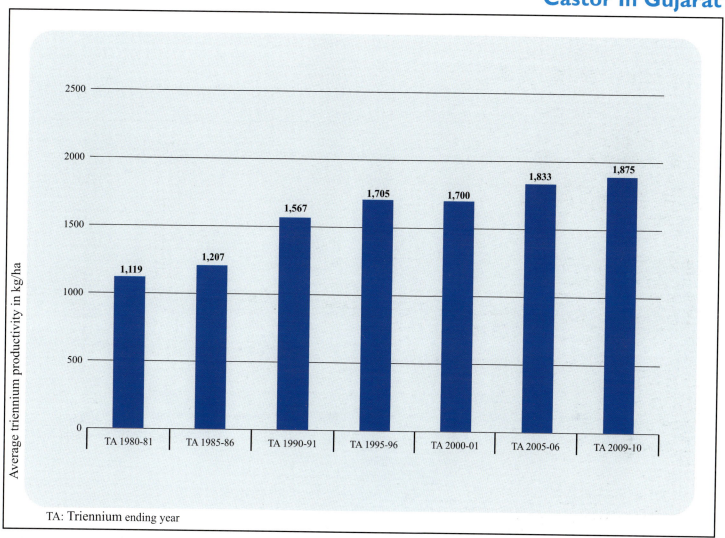

Source: Agriculture University, Dantiwada, 2010

Increase In Productivity Of Cotton (in lint) In Gujarat

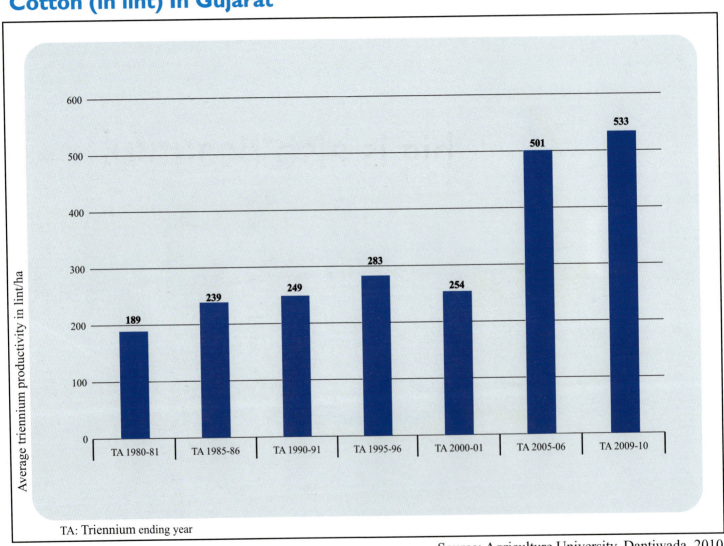

TA: Triennium ending year

Source: Agriculture University, Dantiwada, 2010

Big Is Also Beautiful (Sardar Sarovar Project)

Overflowing Sardar Sarovar Dam

Sardar Sarovar Project of Gujarat has been one of the most talked about large dam projects in the world in recent decades. Mired in controversies, political mismanagement and financial troubles, I inherited the project in an atmosphere of despair and hopelessness. Managing the rehabilitation in coordination with other neighbouring State Governments, satisfying the administrative and quasi-judicial mechanisms established by various judicial pronouncements and arranging for a high dose of finance on a continuous basis, was a task which consumed much of my attention during initial years.

Big Is Also Beautiful (Sardar Sarovar Project)

A View Of Sardar Sarovar Dam Spillway

Dam Height And Storage Increase In Sardar Sarovar Project

Stage	2003	2004	2006	Ultimate
Height	100 m	110.64 m	121.92 m	138.68 m
Gross Storage	2,602.6 MCM (2.11 MAF)	3,700 MCM (3.00 MAF)	5,265.8 MCM (4.27 MAF)	9,460 MCM (7.7 MAF)
Live (Usable) Storage	-- --	-- --	1,565.8 MCM (1.27 MAF)	5,800 MCM (4.75 MAF)

Source: Sardar Sarovar Narmada Nigam Limited, 2009

With a concerted strategy and satisfactory compliance of the project obligations in terms of rehabilitation of project affected persons and environmental measures, we were able to ensure the raising of the dam height to 100 m in 2003, 110.64 m in 2004 and 121.92 m in 2006. This facilitated a much higher increase in storage of Narmada waters.

Big Is Also Beautiful (Sardar Sarovar Project)

Inter-basin Transfer Of Narmada Water

Raising the dam height and the corresponding increase in the storage capacity have significantly improved the water supply and hydropower generation. The real benefits of the project which were awaited for almost 15 years have now started flowing. Diversion of Narmada waters to the main canal of the project (world's largest lined irrigation canal) was just 705 MCM in the year 2001, but it spectacularly increased to 5,195 MCM in 2003 and to 6,194 MCM in 2004. Although we deliberately decreased the water flow in subsequent years due to consecutive good monsoons, it remained to the extent of 4,201 MCM in 2005, 4,292 MCM in 2008 and 5,870 MCM in 2009. We also completed the construction of the main canal in the year 2008 and started water supplies to our neighbouring State – Rajasthan – in March 2008, fulfilling real objective of this project as an Inter-State River Project.

Not only this, with the command area being covered to the extent of around 500,000 ha, we have significantly interlinked many rivers by the interbasin transfer of Narmada waters using the Sardar Sarovar Canal Network.

Narmada water has been released in the dry beds of Heran, Orsang, Karad, Dhadhar, Mahi, Saidak, Mohar, Shedhi, Watrak, Meshwo, Khari, Sabarmati and Saraswati rivers. The ecology and water quality of these rivers have drastically improved

Thus Flows The Narmada Water In 458 km Long Canal

over the last couple of years. In addition to minor rivers, around 700 village tanks have also been filled-up with Narmada water as part of drought management measures, which has substantially improved the water availability for irrigation purpose in these villages.

Another long pending issue was that of operationalising the 250 MW Canal Head Power House (for want of required water head in the reservoir). We operationalised this power house in August, 2004, and thereafter a river bed power house of 1,200 MW capacity was also put into operation in a phased manner starting from February, 2005 to June, 2006. The hydropower generation that commenced in Sardar Sarovar Project since August 2004, has resulted in generation of 15,070 million kWh of electricity till March, 2010.

Impact Of Narmada Water On Quality Of Other River Waters (Annual Average)

Name of River	Place of Measurement	Index for water quality							
		pH		Dissolved Oxygen		Bio Chemical Oxygen Demand		Chemical Oxygen Demand	
		2002-03	2006-07	2002-03	2006-07	2002-03	2006-07	2002-03	2006-07
Sabarmati	Vasna-Narol Bridge	6.2 to 8.5	7.42	1.13	2.3	78	84	214	205
	Railway Bridge Ahmedabad	6.9 to 8.4	7.95	4.12	6.0	22	4.3	72	27
Shedhi	Kheda	7.3 to 8.2	7.98	8.36	6.1	9	7	38	26
Mahi	Vasad	7.6 to 8.8	8.26	5.73	8.4	4	2.5	--	10
Dhadhar	Kothvada	7.81	8.03	0.6	8.3	41	4.1	--	10

Except pH all the parameters are in mg/l

Source: Gujarat Pollution Control Board Annual Report, 2008

Environment – Sardar Sarovar Project

- Catchment Area Treatment in 27,204 ha in forest area and another 1,953 ha in non-forest area.
- Compensatory Afforestation in 4,650 ha of non-forest area and 9,300 ha in forest area.
- Dam vicinity area plantation – 550 ha
- Canal side plantation – 4,120 ha
- Satellite imageries of the year 2006 reveal increase of 21.6% in dense forest, 4% increase in open forest and reduction of degraded forests by 26.57% as compared to the year 1986.
- Mangrove plantation in 110 ha area in the downstream of the Dam.
- Gully plugging 1,156,773 m^3, Brushwood Plugging in 34,491 m^3, Contour Dyke in 17,437 m.
- 131 Permanent Checkdams, 436 Temporary Checkdams and 21 Checkwalls.

Compensatory Afforestation

Environmental Enrichment By Sardar Sarovar Project

I find the inter-linkages between water and energy very fascinating in the case of Sardar Sarovar Project. The wide availability of Narmada water from Sardar Sarovar has led to intangible benefits in terms of virtual savings of electricity that would otherwise have been consumed to draw this amount of water from ground water resources. This has further led to virtual savings of water that would have been consumed in generation of this electricity through Thermal Power Generation. The recorded pattern of electricity consumption in Gujarat, in the year 2000-01, showed that the agricultural sector consumed the highest

share at 45.12% whereas the industrial sector ranked second with 28.59% consumption. But the situation changed by the year 2008-09 due to concurrent emphasis that my Government gave to Sardar Sarovar Project as well as Micro Water Harvesting Sector. Therefore, the consumption of electricity by agricultural sector drastically reduced to 21.10% leaving scope for enhanced consumption by industries. With this, their share in consumption increased to around 35.26% in the year 2008-09.

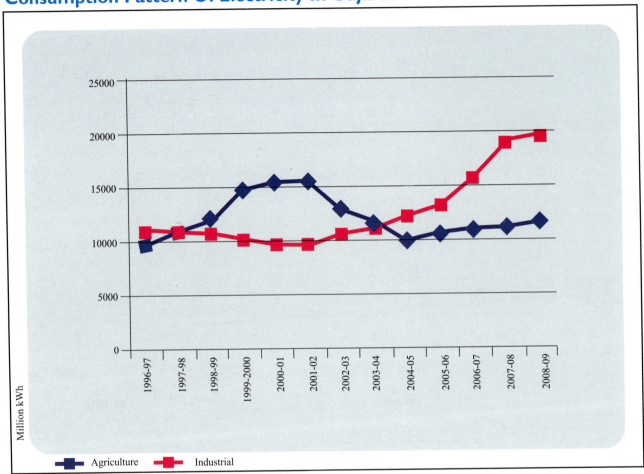

Eco-friendly Power From Sardar Sarovar Project

Year	Generation of Electricity (Million kWh)	Year	Generation of Electricity (Million kWh)
2004-05	263.257	2007-08	4,435.692
2005-06	1,951.782	2008-09	2,317.673
2006-07	3,600.082	2009-10	2,501.327

Source: Sardar Sarovar Narmada Nigam Limited, 2010

Canal Head Power House (250 MW) SSP, Kevadia Colony

Now it is clear that if the earlier trend of consumption had continued, the agricultural sector would have required around 25,091 million kWh in 2008-09 (at 45.12% of total consumption). But the actual consumption had been brought down to 11,733 million kWh, which suggests a saving of about 13,358 million kWh per year. Technically this may be attributed to the combined effects of (a) no more need to pump groundwater in many areas and (b) lower pumping requirements due to recharge of aquifers (where pumping could not be avoided altogether). Such savings must have increased gradually over these years, the total of which could be assessed at 53,432 million kWh. Therefore, the total assessed benefits of electricity would aggregate to 68,502 (=15,070 + 53,432) million kWh.

Now extending this argument further, the generation of this much electricity by Thermal mode would have further required 445.226 MCM of water. And to draw this water from groundwater resources would have further necessitated electricity consumption. Therefore, due to water and energy linkages, savings in one sector have led to savings in another and ultimately have led to equivalent savings in CO_2 emission to the extent of 15.459 million tonnes. What better example of emission reduction could there be?

Machine Hall Of River Bed Power House (1200 MW)

Contribution Of Sardar Sarovar Project In Reduction Of GHG

Particulars	Generation / Savings in Electricity (Million kWh)	Equivalent Savings in Coal (Million Tonnes)	Equivalent Savings in CO_2 Emission (Million Tonnes)	Equivalent Suspended Particulate Matter (Tonnes)	Equivalent Sulphur Dioxide Emission (Metric Tonnes)
Hydropower at RBPH & CHPH	15,070.00 (till March, 2010)	10.549	3.364	164,836	387,291
Electricity saved due to water supply	13,358.00 per year (2008-09) so total 53,432.00	37.402	11.938	584,440	1,373,175
Electricity virtually saved by not fetching 445.226 MCM water for above power generation by thermal mode	711.51	0.498	0.157	7,783	18,286
Total	69,213.51	48.449	15.459	757,059	1,778,752

Note : RBPH - River Bed Power House
CHPH - Canal Head Power House

Source: Sardar Sarovar Narmada Nigam Limited, 2010

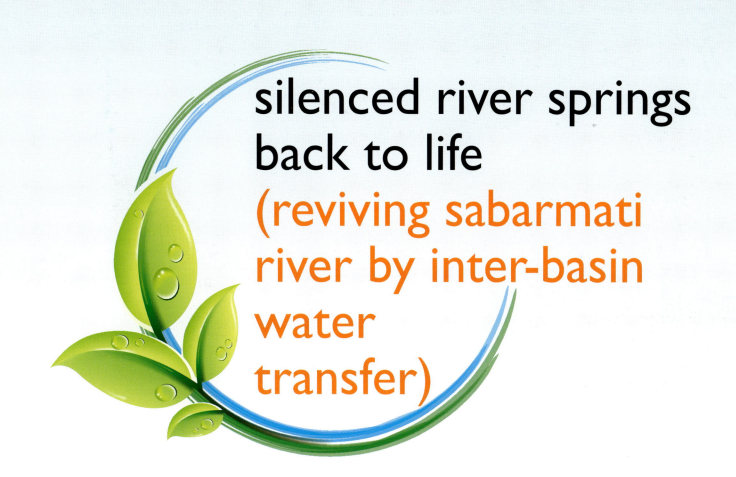

Silenced River Springs Back To Life (Reviving Sabarmati River By Inter-basin Water Transfer)

One day while passing through one of the bridges of Sabarmati River that connects eastern Ahmedabad with its ever expanding western side, I saw a few children playing cricket in the dry riverbed. A thought struck my mind with lightening speed. "Oh! this generation, if asked about Sabarmati River, will only term it as large play ground, completely unaware of the rich ecology and bustling water resources that it once possessed.

Sabarmati River Front Development Project
Ahmedabad, Gujarat

Silenced River Springs Back To Life (Reviving Sabarmati River By Inter-basin Water Transfer)

No! we should not deprive our children of the eternal happiness they would derive from flowing water and the adult denizens of the city of pleasure of living by the river side", I said unto myself.

And then I realised that since long Sabarmati River has been subjected to severe pressure and abuse owing to fast pace of urban and industrial growth of city of Ahmedabad with over four million inhabitants. On the other hand, in absence of regular releases of water from Dharoi dam in upstream, this river practically remained without any source of water. Due to this, for years, the river banks remained neglected and characterized by unimaginative and

Construction Of River Front

unplanned development. Its banks and bed remaining dry most of the time, provided a place to stay and source of livelihood for many poor citizens. These river bank slums had been disastrously flood prone and lacked basic infrastructure services. The slums located along the river bed had always been a major impediment to efficient management of monsoon floods in the river. Sewage contaminated the storm water outfalls and the dumping of industrial waste posed a major health and environmental hazard. The river water samples taken in November 2003 showed a high level of Bio Oxygen Demand, Chemical Oxygen Demand, Chlorides, Sulphates, Total Dissolved Solids, Suspended Solids, Fecal Coliform and very less Dissolved Oxygen,

all of which cause water-borne diseases and have an adverse impact on aquatic life.

"How to bring life back to this historical river?", I asked myself. I knew that there was no other perennial and dependable source of water which could turn this river back to flowing state except Narmada water. Fortunately, the Narmada main canal was ready to transfer the Narmada water to the river Sabarmati after travelling a distance of 230 km. With the Narmada main canal duly completed to bring water to this point and with the already provided escape structure, it was an ideal arrangement to operationalise the inter-basin transfer of Narmada water, I thought.

Retaining Wall At River Front

Silenced River Springs Back To Life (Reviving Sabarmati River By Inter-basin Water Transfer)

Inter-basin Transfer Of Narmada Waters Into Sabarmati

On the Narmada Main Canal, an escape structure with discharge carrying capacity of 450 m³ per second (15,890 cubic feet per second) was constructed during 1998-2001, which cost ₹ 60 million*. The primary objective of this escape structure was to safely release the canal water to Sabarmati river in the event of any sort of mismatch between the demand and supply which could cause a potential threat to the safety of the canal. However, its potential to bring about inter-basin transfer of Narmada water

*1 US$ ≅ ₹ 47

was untapped, for the simple reason that the constructed dam height and created storage potential in Sardar Sarovar were not conducive to such a large-scale diversion of water. With the stage-wise increase in the Sardar Sarovar dam height and associated enhancement in available storage, this escape structure became a perennial source of water for Sabarmati river. This not only quenched the thirst of the city of Ahmedabad, by effective utilisation of surplus water from Narmada, but even the French Wells in the riverbed got rejuvenated. With three radial gates of the size 7.0 m x 8.3 m, it was now possible to release regulated discharge in the dry riverbed of Sabarmati and thus the dream of many to see the Sabarmati river in spate

Illumination Signifying Revival Of Sabarmati

finally came true. During last three years, on an average, 600 to 1,200 MCM of water was released every year in the dry bed of river Sabarmati, which gets stored in a stretch of 10.6 km – right upto Vasna Barrage.

Having ensured that round the year inter-basin transfer of Narmada water will make the river Sabarmati independent of the vagaries of nature during monsoon, I decided that appropriate development of the riverfront could turn the river into a major asset, which would improve the quality of environment and life in Ahmedabad, improve the efficiency of its infrastructure, conserve the places of heritage importance, and create an opportunity for recreation and hospitality industry. However, as usual my direct intervention was required to cut through the bureaucratic web for transfer of the 202.79 ha land to Ahmedabad Municipal Corporation for the execution of River Front Project by Sabarmati River Front Development Corporation Limited (SRFDCL). And thereafter, the project took off beautifully.

Earth-Filling At River Front

Perennial Water Body

- The ambitious project involves creating embankments on both sides of Sabarmati river and developing a 10.6 km stretch of riverfront along each of the banks – from upstream of Subhash Bridge to Vasna Barrage. This stretch would become a perennial water body after the completion of the River Front Development Project.

- In this project, separate intercepter line is to be laid on both sides of the river for disposal of mixed sewer that would result in better quality of water and save aquatic life.

- The project will also provide protection against 500,000 cusec flood, which will not only eliminate the annual flooding of low lying areas but would also prevent evacuation of nearly 10,000 Slum Households, located on riverbanks as well as the villages on downstream of Vasna Barrage. It would at the same time prevent the scouring of farm lands.

- Due to heavy drawl of ground water during past many years, there has been a depletion of ground water table by 2.0 m annually. But implementation of SRFDCL project would result in recharging of ground water aquifer.

- 202.79 ha of land is being reclaimed and getting utilised for green environment development, which would reduce greenhouse gas emission.

Land Use In River Front Development Project

Land Uses	Area (ha)	Area (%)
Roads	39.30	19.38
Gardens	76.78	37.86
Promenades	32.40	15.98
Informal Markets	3.51	1.73
Commercial / Residential Areas	29.40	14.50
Public Utilities / Extension of Public Facilities	18.96	9.35
Residual / Unallocated	2.44	1.20
Total	202.79	100.00

Source: Sabarmati River Front Development Corporation Limited, 2009

In Search Of Better Alternatives (Panam High Level Canal Project)

During the last couple of years I have consciously tried to ensure that in water resources development more environment friendly solutions with lesser carbon footprints are preferred over the ones that are more technology driven, with higher carbon footprints. A very interesting example is the recently executed Panam High Level Canal Project.

3.3 km Long Tunnel - Panam High Level Canal Project

In Search Of Better Alternatives (Panam High Level Canal Project)

Panam Dam
District Panchmahals, Gujarat

Panam dam was constructed across Panam river in Central Gujarat (Panchmahals District) in 1978, with irrigation command area covering more than 130 villages (36,405 ha) and also providing drinking water to around 330,000 people. It has a small canal based hydro power station of 2 MW capacity.

In Search Of Better Alternatives (Panam High Level Canal Project)

Effectively, the requirement of around 200,000 people is fulfilled by this multipurpose project. However, since its inception the project suffered from one major deficiency – Panam main canal, a 100 km long contour canal, served only the command area that fell to its right side while the farmers on the higher grounds of this command area were deprived of irrigation due to difficult and inconvenient topography.

During one of my visits to the area, a few years back, there were strong representations of these farmers who expressed their concerns. Ever since then, I had been weighing the various alternatives that were brought before me as solutions.

*1 US$ ≅ ₹ 47

Panam Spillway
District Panchmahals, Gujarat

Panchmahals District comprises of geological terrain of Aravali hills and along the alignment of the high level main canal there sits a big hillock which forms the main barrier to the increase in command area.

The first alternative was to dig an open canal (channel) with around 60 m depth and with an average cutting of 36 m, at a cost of ₹ 1,500 million.* This would have also necessitated acquisition of around 35 ha of private and reserved forest lands, felling of 39,000 trees and displacement of 22 families.

The channel cutting of around 4.8 million m³ would have necessitated consumption of 3.23 million litres of fossil fuel (diesel), etc., for excavators and other machineries.

In Search Of Better Alternatives (Panam High Level Canal Project)

The second alternative was lifting water from the reservoir through pumping by laying down pipelines and constructing pumping stations at a cost of ₹ 1,300 million*. For irrigating 18,000 ha we would have required lifting 800 cusecs water at 55 m height for 80 days. This would have amounted to the use of 2,000 MW power which in turn would have led to additional emission of 3.57 million tCO_2 every year.

Considering very high carbon footprints, human displacement and direct loss of forest lands, I decided not to go in for these alternatives. Instead, I chose to get an irrigation tunnel constructed at a cost of around ₹ 558.40 million*. This water carrying tunnel is the first of its kind in Gujarat and one of the very few existing in the country. With a length of 3,362 m, 6.60 m bed width and 6.60 m height, it has 800 cubic feet per second discharge capacity. By making this tunnel, we would provide irrigation to 18,000 ha of land benefiting around 125,000 people at no extra submergence and no displacement of persons. We would also be utilising only the surplus water from the existing reservoir. As an additional advantage, the nearby wells, around 60 village tanks and 500 checkdams are being interlinked for recharge with the canal work, providing irrigation in an additional area of 2,000 ha. It has been a win-win situation since surplus water in the existing reservoir has been diverted at minimum environmental and human costs. I treat this as a positive step in my search of better alternatives for development of Gujarat.

*1 US$ ≅ ₹ 47

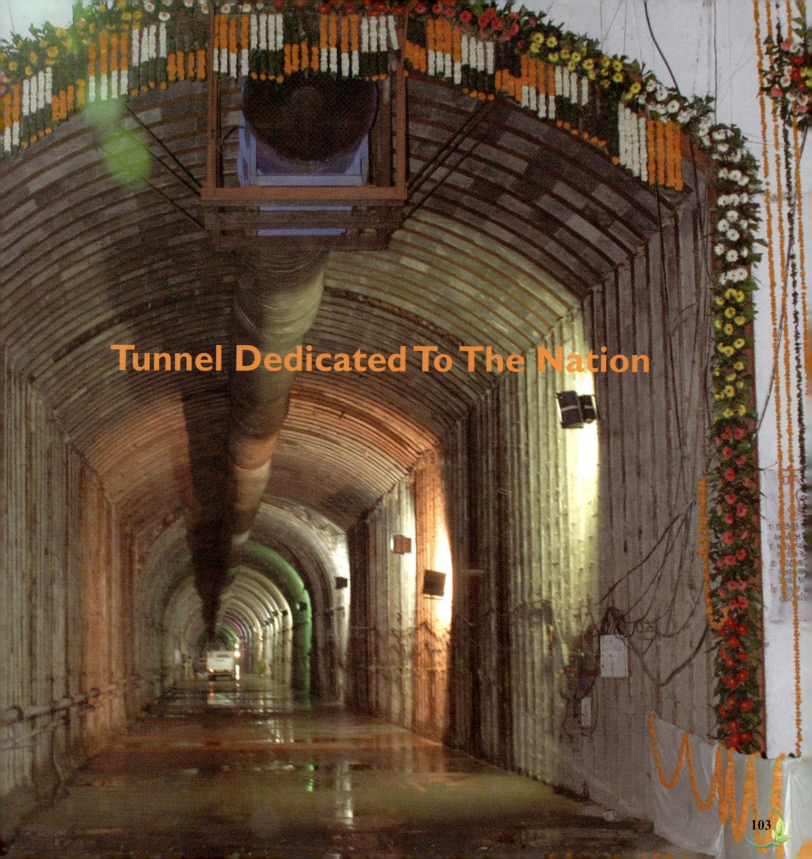

In Search Of Better Alternatives (Panam High Level Canal Project)

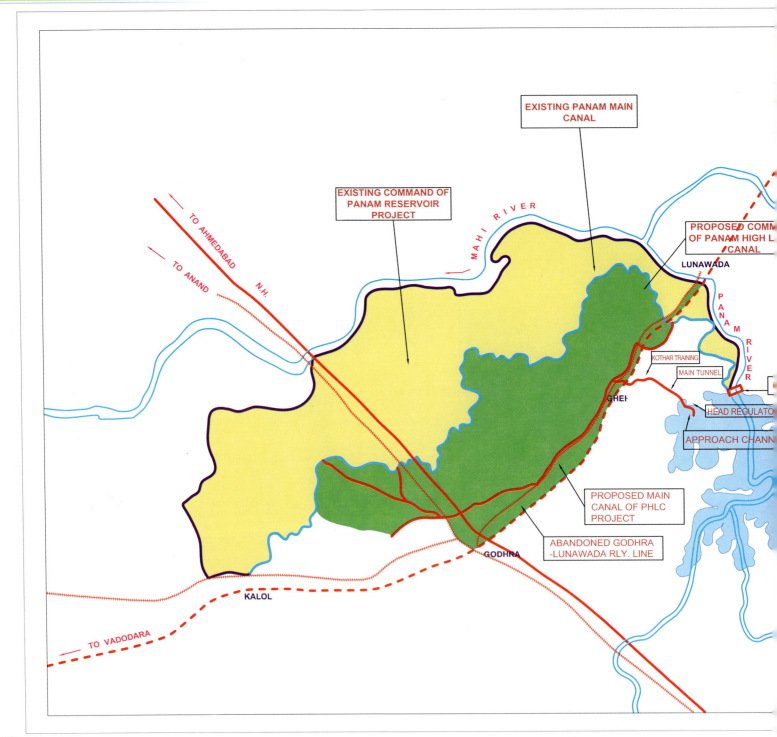

Layout of Panam High Level Canal Project

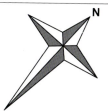

LEGEND

1.	KADANA DAM SITE	
2.	PANAM DAM SITE	
3.	BHADAR DAM SITE	
4.	EXISTING PANAM MAIN CANAL	
9.	COMMAND OF EXISTING PANAM MAIN CANAL	
5.	PANAM SUBMERGENCE AREA	
6.	PANAM HIGH LEVEL CANAL (LEFT AND RIGHT BRANCH)	
7.	NATIONAL/STATE HIGHWAY ROAD	
8.	RAILWAYS	
9.	COMMAND OF PANAM HIGH LEVEL CANAL	

In Search Of Better Alternatives (Panam High Level Canal Project)

Tunnel Of Hope

Panam High Level Canal - Alternatives Considered

36 m Deep Open Canal

Canal section having 6.6 m bed width and 3 m berm on both sides at 6 m interval and inside slope of 1:1 in 6 m soil portion and 0.5:1 in rest of soft/hard rock strata is considered as an average section for 36 m deep canal.

Excavation Quantity = 4.80 million m^3

Considering one excavator with hauling equipments consuming 14 litre diesel per hour and having output of 500 m^3 per day.

Diesel required per 1 m^3 excavation

= (14 x 24) / 500

= 0.672 litre

Total diesel required in this case

= 4.8 million m^3 x 0.672 litre per m^3

= 3.23 million litres

55 m Lift From Reservoir

Quantity of water required for
18,000 ha = 150 MCM
= 5,580 Mcft
= 5,580 x 11.574 day cusecs
= 64,583 day cusecs

No. of days of Pumping
64,583 day cusecs to be lifted at the rate of 800 cusecs per day i.e. 64,583 / 800
= 80 days

Electricity Requirement
1cusecs for 33 m lift need 24.24 HP
So that 64,583 day cusecs lifting for 55 m need = 2,609,153 HP
= 1,946,428 kW

Total power required to lift 800 cusecs
for 80 days = 2,000 MW

Energy required per day to lift 800 cusecs
= (2,000 x 10^3 kW)/ 80 days
= 25,000 kW/day
= 25,000/24 kWh
= 1,041 kWh @ Head Regulator

O & M Cost per day
At ₹ 4 per kWh with other M&R
= ₹ 100,000* per day

Coal consumption
= 0.67 MT/ MW x 2,000 MW
= 1,340 MT

*1 US$ ≅ ₹ 47

Traffic Congestion
Ahmedabad, Gujarat

With the burgeoning population (around 4.5 million) in Ahmedabad city, around eight hundred thousand passengers are ferried every day through a fleet of over one thousand Ahmedabad Municipal Transport Service (AMTS) buses and around 1.9 million private vehicles of all kinds ply on Ahmedabad roads. Therefore, enormous traffic and its congestion is a major source of greenhouse gas emission in Ahmedabad city.

Reducing Urban Warming

BRTS Station
Ahmedabad, Gujarat

To ease the traffic congestion and simultaneously reduce the GHG emission, we have carefully planned and executed the Bus Rapid Transit System (BRTS) at a cost of around ₹ 9,820 million*. This would ultimately reduce the movement of 400,000 vehicles per day and carry 100,000 additional passengers through BRTS buses over and above AMTS buses. It has been estimated by the Centre for Environmental Planning & Technology (CEPT) University in Ahmedabad, that there would be a net reduction of 37,000 tonnes GHG per annum (mainly CO_2 and NOx) as a result of this massive project.

*1 US$ ≅ ₹ 47

Reducing Urban Warming

In addition to this, more than a dozen flyovers are being executed in Ahmedabad city which would facilitate easy transit of around 200,000 vehicles, ultimately leading to emission reduction.

Flyover
Ahmedabad, Gujarat

Reducing Urban Warming

Flyover
Surat, Gujarat

Similar efforts in Surat, rated as the fastest growing metropolitan city in the State, have resulted in substantial improvements in air quality and reduction of average concentration of air pollutants at different locations of flyovers.

Ahmedabad drops to 66th Rank from 4th Rank in polluted cities in India.

The Central Pollution Control Board (CPCB), New Delhi, has been generating the ambient air quality data through various monitoring sources in different urban areas of the country. The ambient air quality with respect to Respirable Suspended Particulate Matter (RSPM) is one of the most critical parameters being monitored and has been a matter of concern in residential locations of Indian urban areas. In the year 2001, the annual average concentration of RSPM levels in residential locations of Ahmedabad was reported to be 198 µg/m^3 which was fourth highest concentration in the cities of India for which the reports were published by CPCB.

As per a recent report of CPCB, the annual average of RSPM in the year 2007, in Ahmedabad was 86 µg/m^3 which was 53rd amongst the 85 cities for which data were published by the CPCB. Further, according to year 2008 data the RSPM levels in residential areas of Ahmedabad was 80 µg/m^3 improving its rank to the 66th position amongst the 90 cities for which data were published by them.

Reducing Urban Warming

Changes In Air Quality In Surat City (µg/m³)

Location Details		SPM	RSPM	SOx	NOx	CO	HC
Varachha Road FOB Reduction of pollutant level at Minibazar	From the level of Khand Bazar	34.38%	33.15%	29.54%	39.0%	29.61%	26.67%
		121	61	9.6	18.8	610	0.4
	From the level of Kapodra	105	40	6	10.2	380	0.2
		31.25%	24.54%	20.76%	25.76%	20.77%	15.38%
Ring Road FOB Reduction of pollutant level at Textile market	From the level of Udhana Darwaja	36.64%	40.78%	37.83%	40.94%	19.0%	25.0%
		144	73	14.3	21.3	420	0.4
	From the level of Kapodra	115	38	9.6	18.2	380	0.3
		31.59%	26.39%	29.0%	36.77%	17.51%	20.0%

Source: Surat Municipal Corporation, 2009

At Majuragate Junction Surat Station

Average Concentration Of Air Pollutant (µg/m³) In Surat City

Station (Nana Varachha FOB)	Date	SO$_2$	H$_2$S	CO	RSPM	NOx
Starting (Surat side)	22.4.10	69	60.22	3,400	152	76
Middle (Underbridge at junction)	22.4.10	36	40.52	1,940	120	30
End Point (Kamrej side)	22.4.10	71	65.44	4,000	157	71

Source: Surat Municipal Corporation, 2010

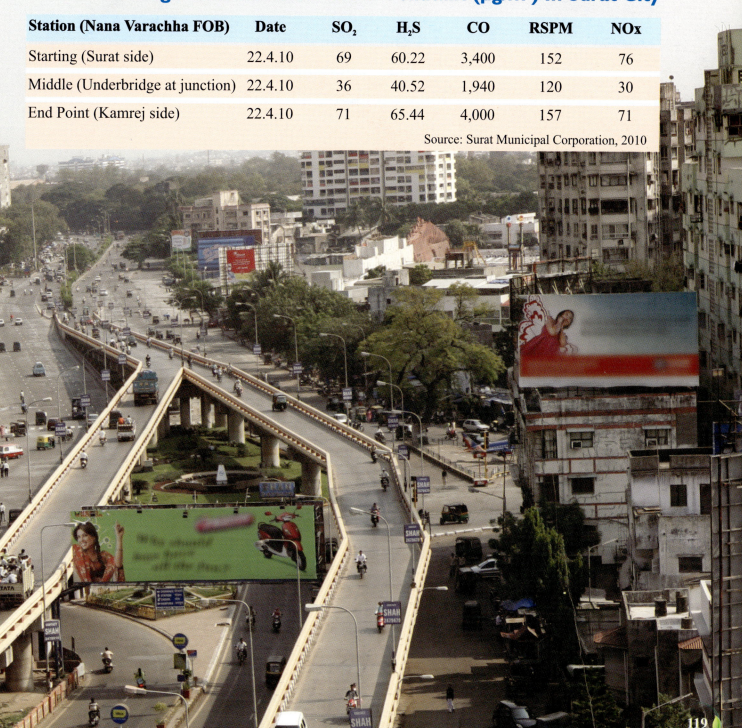

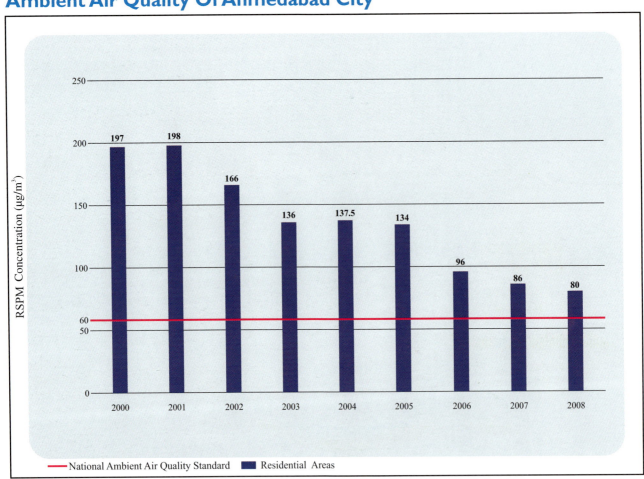

Source: Central Pollution Control Board, 2009

Switchover To Gaseous Green

Considering the fact that Climate Change is not only an environmental issue but also a developmental issue, we have adopted a forward looking and development oriented approach. We have decided to introduce clean fuel mechanism in the State of Gujarat by expanding oil and gas value chain. A State Wide Gas Grid has been planned to provide clean and green fuel even to the remote areas of the State. Around 1,500 km long High Pressure Gas Pipeline (HPGP) has been laid and commissioned. This pipeline passes through 15 districts of Gujarat and caters to the requirements of power sector, fertilisers, chemicals, small and medium industries, ceramic and glass industries, etc. Additionally 800 km of high pressure pipeline is under construction and Gujarat is the only State in the country to have a State Wide Gas Grid.

Completed	1446.00 Km.
Under Execution	450.00 Km.
Under Development	368.00 Km.

Gas Grid Development – Gujarat

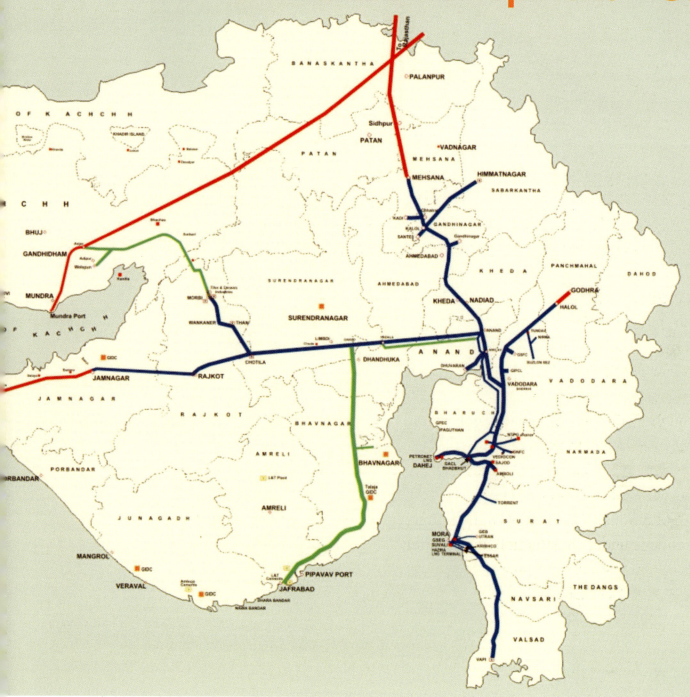

Switchover To Gaseous Green

GSPC Gas Filling Station
District Ahmedabad, Gujarat

City Gas Distribution Project

Gujarat State Petroleum Corporation (GSPC) embarked upon an ambitious plan of city gas distribution envisaging supply of natural gas to various households, automobile segments, commercial establishments and small scale industries located across Gujarat State. This project also aims at setting up Compressed Natural Gas (CNG) stations at various locations which replaces highly polluting fuels like coal, furnace oil, Liquefied Petroleum Gas (LPG), etc., in small industrial zones with environment friendly natural gas and thereby reducing the levels of CO_2 emission. Pilot CNG stations at Hazira and domestic gas connections in the same location were established in the year 2003 and later attracted several private sector players in city gas distribution project. This has been received by villagers as a boon since they no longer have to trek a few kilometers every day for collecting firewood. There are more than 400,000 domestic connections spread across various cities and towns of Gujarat and it is planned to increase their number upto two million during next couple of years. Establishment of CNG stations to cater to the demand of automobile sector has led to conversion of around 200,000 auto-rickshaws, cars and other vehicles to CNG reducing consumption of diesel and petrol and also reducing GHG emission.

Switchover To Gaseous Green

CNG Auto Rickshaw
Ahmedabad, Gujarat

Following table calculates reduction of CO_2 emission by reducing fossil fuels through use of natural gas in the State of Gujarat:

Sr.No.	Segment	Gas Flow MMSCMD	Reduction of tCO_2 emission
1.	Domestic	0.39	67,853
2.	Industrial	57.00	23,165,722
3.	Transportation	1.17	204,535
	Total	58.56	23,438,110

Source: Gujarat State Petroleum Corporation, 2009

GSPC Krishna Godavari Rig

Pandit Deendayal Petroleum University (PDPU)

Gujarat State Petroleum Corporation (GSPC) has established Pandit Deendayal Petroleum University to address the need for training human resources for energy sector. In this University the School of Solar Energy was setup to conduct teaching and research in order to provide viable solutions in the areas of solar thermal energy, photovoltaic and other energy systems, energy storage and rational use of energy. Gujarat Energy Research & Management Institute (GERMI), Research & Innovation Centre, has initiated steps to establish Renewable Energy Research and Environment and Climate Change Wing. The Climate Change initiative of PDPU is also planning to collaborate with the Climate Change initiative of London School of Economics.

From Carbon Credits To Green Credits

Clean Development Mechanism (CDM) represents a challenging opportunity for my State to participate in addressing a global concern for which we may not be directly responsible. At the same time it also addresses our socio-economic development priorities.

Gujarat Fluorochemicals Plant
District Panchmahals, Gujarat

From Carbon Credits To Green Credits

Green Belt Development
Common Effluent Treatment Plant
District Valsad, Gujarat

International regulatory system for CDM, however, being a project focused mechanism, has its own limitations. For instance, we have in place a number of projects and policies (enumerated in different sections of this book) that would directly or indirectly help combat Climate Change. Under CDM's current approach it would, however, be difficult to get credits for our efforts. The recognition of public sector projects under the current CDM guidelines is comparatively difficult vis-à-vis private sector projects. Public sector investment is primarily scattered. There are many projects in different parts of the State depending on the local needs. If they are bundled together, high cost of project development and validation procedure make such projects difficult to be taken up for CDM. The programmatic CDM, even though well-defined, has not been able to take off and no validators in India are willing to take up such projects. It should be appreciated that public sector projects contribute to sustainable development of the State and it is required that CDM procedure should be broad based in order to encourage such public sector projects/policies.

The total number of Certified Emission Reductions (CERs) already earned in Gujarat State by industries are 32.896 million out of which, 0.414 million CERs are from public sector and 32.482 million CERs are from private sector (till 1st July, 2010). The number of CERs being earned annually (an average of crediting period) in Gujarat State by industries are 13.516 million CERs. As per the total CERs issued till 1st July, 2010 in the country, Gujarat is the highest rated and has generated 41.58% of total issued CERs in India.

CDM - At A Glance In India

State	Total No. of CDM projects (registered, under review and pipeline)	Estimated GHG displacement in tonnage/year (in thousands)	No. of projects registered with UNFCCC	Total CERs issued till 1st July, 2010 (in thousands)
Maharashtra	232	12,822	62	1,319
Tamil Nadu	217	9,525	60	6,836
Karnataka	189	11,577	62	10,181
Gujarat	176	26,458	42	32,896
Andhra Pradesh	121	11,468	51	3,639
All India	1,704	149,131	513	79,116

Source: Gujarat Urban Development Corporation, 2010

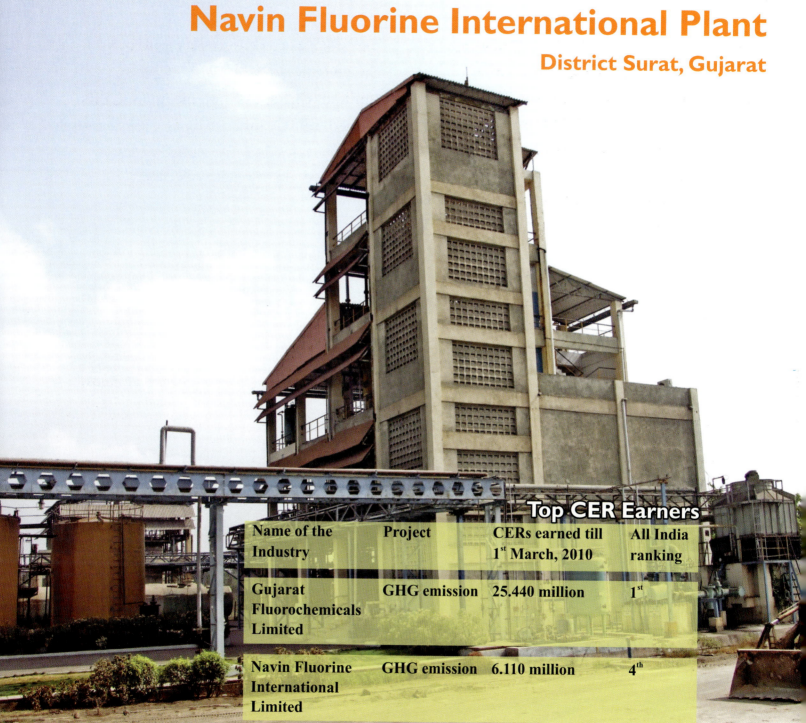

Navin Fluorine International Plant
District Surat, Gujarat

Top CER Earners

Name of the Industry	Project	CERs earned till 1st March, 2010	All India ranking
Gujarat Fluorochemicals Limited	GHG emission	25.440 million	1st
Navin Fluorine International Limited	GHG emission	6.110 million	4th

Source: Gujarat Urban Development Corporation, 2010

The estimated annual GHG displacement by way of earning CERs is 26.458 million tCO_2 for all projects registered, under review and in pipeline in Gujarat. The estimated GHG displacement is 32.862 million tCO_2 based on total CERs issued till 1st July, 2010 from registered projects in Gujarat.

I have, however, not been too comfortable with Carbon Credit system since it kind of reflects 'wrong doer's penance' in monetary terms.

CDM Project In Surat City

Surat Municipal Corporation (SMC) has undertaken CDM projects to utilise methane gas, which is generated during sewage treatment. It has done so by installing a Sewage Gas based Power Plant. The project is designed to generate sewage gas by treating the sludge generated from primary and secondary clarifier of sewage in an anaerobic processing system (Digester) so as to restrict the atmospheric emission of methane gas. At the same time methane gas is recovered without leak in the atmosphere.

The electricity generated from the utilisation of sewage gas in the gas engine is used for captive purpose. Thus greenhouse gas reduction by fossil fuel consumption reduction for grid power supply equivalency is, therefore, possible.

SMC commissioned India's first Sewage Gas based Power Plant (SGPP) of 0.5 MW capacity at Anjana Sewage Treatment Plant (STP) in 2003. It also commissioned three SGPP, each of 1.0 MW capacity in year 2008 at different STPs. These Power Plants have generated more than 12.888 million kWh electricity and reduced the GHG emission equivalent to 52,100 tCO_2. For registration under CDM, these projects fall under the small scale in following categories:

- TYPE III.H. Methane recovery in wastewater.
- TYPE I.D: Grid connected renewable electricity generation

The annual expected CERs from these two categories are 39,630 and 16,624 respectively.

Gas Holder, CDM Project
District Surat, Gujarat

From Carbon Credits To Green Credits

CDM Project
District Surat, Gujarat

From Carbon Credits To Green Credits

There is a need to develop a more positive approach. With this in mind I exhorted my officials to develop the innovative scheme of 'Green Credits'.

Sometimes the socio-economic and infrastructure development projects necessitate the acquisition of lands that have been declared as protected under Forest Conservation Act, 1980 in India.

Development of compensatory afforestation after the non-forest usage may take many years and till then there are bound to be adverse impacts on the environment.

Punit Van – Trees and Constellations

According to Indian astrology, the particular constellation in which a person is born, keeps influencing his life in different ways – good or bad, depending on particular position of that constellation. In order to get rid of the evil influences and to invoke the divine goodness to be bestowed upon him, a person has to perform certain religious rituals. It is also mentioned in our ancient scriptures that if a particular plant that is associated with a definite constellation is planted, nurtured and worshipped, the ill effects of that particular constellation could be neutralised and over a period of time get converted into positive influence. There are 27 constellations and each one of these is associated with one or more plants species.

'Punit Van' is a plantation of trees in the capital city of Gandhinagar signifying an association of trees with constellations, sunsigns, etc. We enhance peoples' awareness of these concepts by way of film shows in the open air theatre there and also by maintaining a nursery of 'theme specific seedlings' for people to obtain plants of their choice and as per their astrological constellations.

Constellation Plantation
Gandhinagar, Gujarat

Constellation Forest

Name of Constellations	Local Name of Plant	Botanical Name of Plant
Ashwini	Zercochla / Kadayo	Strychnos nuxvomica Sterculia urens
Bharni	Amli	Tamarindus indica
Krutica	Udambar	Ficus racemosa
Rohini	Jamun	Syzygium cumini
Mrugshirsh	Khair	Acacia catechu
Adhra	Sisoo	Dalbergia sissoo
Punarvasu	Vans / Bamboo	Bambusa arundinacea
Pushya	Pipal	Ficus religiosa
Ashlesha	Champo	Michelia champaca
Magha	Vad	Ficus benghalensis
Purva-Falguni	Palas / Khakhro	Butea monosperma
Uttar-Falguni	Palaksha / Pipli	Ficus rumphii
Hasta	Juii / Jasmine	Jasminum aurioulatum
Chitra	Bili / Bel	Aegle marmelos
Swati	Arjun sadad / Arjun	Terminalia arjuna
Vishakha	Vikro	Gymnosporia spinosa
Anuradha	Gugal	Commiphora wightii
Jyestha	Semal	Salmalia malabarica (Bombax malabaricum)
Mul	Amaltas / Garmalo	Cassica fistula
Purvashadha	Netar	Calamus rotang
Utrashadha	Kathal / Phanus	Artocarpus integrifolia
Shravan	Oak / Akdo	Callotropis procera
Ghanistha	Sami / Khijdo	Prosopis cineraria
Shat-tara	Kadamb	Anthocephalus cadamba
Purva-Bhadrapad	Aam	Mangifera Indica
Utra-Bhadrapad	Neem	Azadirachta indica
Revi	Mahuva	Madhuca Indica

Zodiac Plantation

English Name Zodiac	Local Name of Zodiac	Local Name	Botanical Name
Aries	Mesh	Umro / Amla	Ficus glomerata / Embelica officinalis
Taurus	Vrushabha	Khair / Jambu	Acacia catechu / Syzygium cumini Ficus glomerata
Gemini	Mithuna	Khair / Bili	Acacia catechu / Aegle marmelos
Cancer	Karkata	Pipal / Bili	Ficus religiosa / Aeglemarmelos
Leo	Simha	Vad / Khakro	Ficus bengalensis / Butea monosperma
Virgo	Kanya	Bili / Jui	Aegle marmelos / Jasminium auriculatum
Libra	Tula	Bili / Arjun	Aegle marmelos Terminalia arjuna
Scorpio	Vrushchika	Gugal	Commiphera Wightii
Sagittarius	Dhanu	Netar	Calmus rotang
Capricorn	Makara	Phanus	Artocarpus intigrifolia
Aquarius	Kumbh	Ambo / Kadam	Mangifera indica Anthocephalus cadamba
Pisces	Meena	Neem / Limdo	Azadirechta indica

Zodiac Plantation
Gandhinagar, Gujarat

From Carbon Credits To Green Credits

Mangrove Species: Rhizophora Mucronata & Avicennia Marina

Sikka Coast, District Jamnagar, Gujarat

Therefore, under the 'Green Credit' scheme the Forest Department of my Government would identify, in advance, possible areas that can be used and prepare a blue print for their afforestation. They would then sign a Memorandum of Understanding (MOU) with potential user agencies, which in turn would provide funds at the disposal of the former for afforestation.

Mangrove Species: Rhizophora Mucronata
Pirotan Island, District Jamnagar, Gujarat

Since this afforestation will take place on private lands under controlled supervision and monitoring of the Forest Department, the latter would then provide credits (certificates) for this. The certificates could be used by the user agency in future at the time of making an application under the Forest Conservation Act, 1980 for the use of forest land for non-forest purposes.

This is a unique scheme prepared for the first time in the country that would create

From Carbon Credits To Green Credits

Mangrove Species: Rhizophora Mucronata & Avicennia Marina
Bhensbid Island, District Jamnagar, Gujarat

Mangroves in Gujarat

Recognising the importance of Mangroves as Carbon sinks, Gujarat has taken up extensive conservation and plantation activities in Mangroves areas. More than 30,000 ha of Mangrove forests have been added during last couple of years in the coastal tracts of Jamnagar, Kutch, Bhavnagar and Anand districts of Gujarat State. Forest Survey of India has undertaken regular mapping of Mangroves cover in the country and according to their estimates, the Mangroves cover in Gujarat has been steadily increasing (proven by satellite data). Our efforts have resulted in having the second largest Mangroves forest cover of 93,600 ha in the country.

Trees And Religious Beliefs

Preservation and conservation of trees, natural flora and fauna have been integrally connected with Indian beliefs, religious notions and way of life. In my early childhood, I distinctly remember how my grandmother forcibly dissuaded one of my uncles from getting into timber trade. The reason was that she equated this trade with butcher's profession. In her system of religious beliefs, cutting of trees was tantamount to the butchering of living beings. My grandmother was a simple semi-literate lady but she possessed a very strong sense of conviction for conservation of nature. Later in life during my visits to Himalayas for self-exploration and self-realisation, I had many occasions to meet a number of spiritually enlightened souls who exhibited unflinching dedication and single minded devotion towards the preservation of nature to the extent of equating it with the worship of God.

Shri Pandurang Shastry Athvale was one of the best known socio-religious preachers in Gujarat. He will be known for many centuries to come for his work in exhorting coastal communities for renunciation of evil social practices. 'Pandurang Dada', as he was known affectionately, went out of his way to establish 'tree temples' in Gujarat in order to generate religious reverence for trees and thereby create a social ethos for conservation of nature. Some communities in Gujarat, on certain instances of tree felling have been observing the same rituals as are performed after death of human beings.

These personal and socio-cultural beliefs have always motivated me to go for massive tree plantations, preventing tree felling as far as possible, incorporating nature conservation and environment protection as an important ingredient in my party's manifesto during elections and even import necessary mechanical tools from Canada, for shifting big grown up trees, if unavoidable developmental requirements made it necessary.

In olden times in India, most cities were protected by a defence wall constructed around its periphery. In recent times in Gujarat, I have been advising urban local bodies to go in for massive tree plantations around the cities to make a defence line against global warming.

From Carbon Credits To Green Credits

Mangrove Species: Ceriops Tagal
Bhensbid Island, District Jamnagar, Gujarat

substantial Carbon sinks and would reduce any time gap for development of extensive plantation after some forest lands are consumed for possible infrastructural activities.

Increase In Mangrove Cover (1998 - 2006, Indicated By Red Tone) Satellite Imagery

October 17, 1998

March 2, 2006

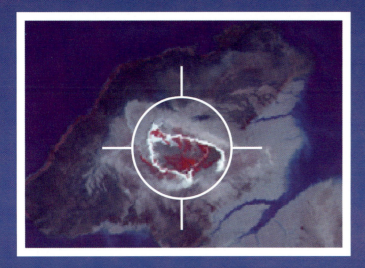
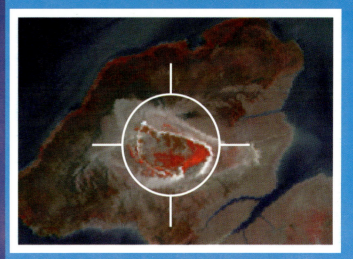

Pirotan Island, Gulf of Kutch, District Jamnagar, Gujarat

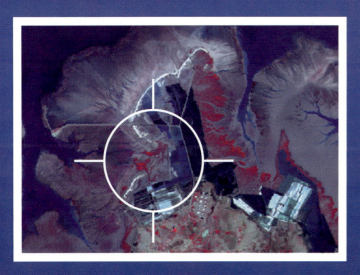

Narara, Gulf of Kutch, District Jamnagar, Gujarat

From Carbon Credits To Green Credits

Increase In Mangrove Cover (1998 - 2006, Indicated By Red Tone) Satellite Imagery

October 17, 1998

March 2, 2006

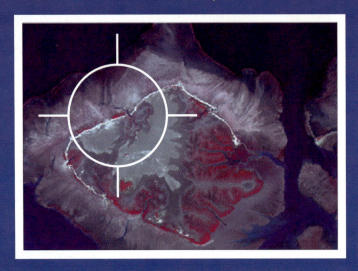
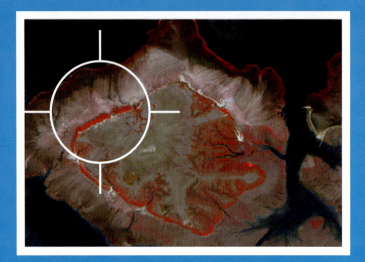

Kalubhar, Gulf of Kutch, District Jamnagar, Gujarat

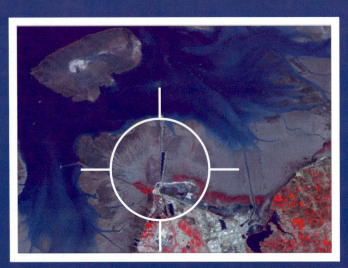

Sikka Coast, Gulf of Kutch, District Jamnagar, Gujarat

Increase In Mangrove Cover (1998 - 2006, Indicated By Red Tone) Satellite Imagery

October 17, 1998

March 2, 2006

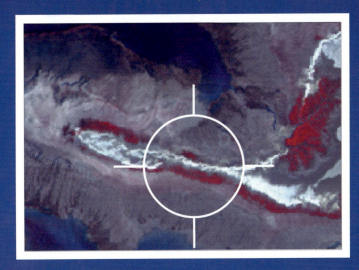

Dedeka-Mundeka Island, Gulf of Kutch, District Jamnagar, Gujarat

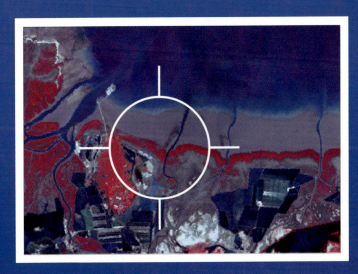
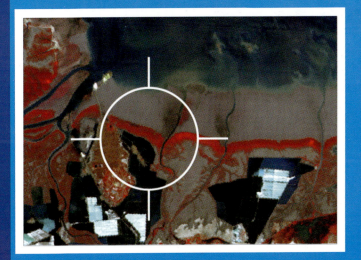

Jamnagar Coastal Area, Gulf of Kutch, Gujarat

Sow trees – Sow earthen pots

We still have traditional method of cooling water in earthen pots sculpted by village potters. Come summers and millions of earthen pots are made and sold in rural, semi urban and even several parts of urban India. Gujarat is no exception to this. However, within one season these pots lose their cooling ability necessitating owners to purchase new ones with the onset of next season. Old ones get thrown away. I have been advocating reuse of these pots by making a small hole at the bottom and filling that with a knot of thread (traditional way of dripping water droplets for ablution of Linga of Lord Shiva in India). If these improvised earthen pots are also buried in ground, leaving their mouths open, next to any sapling; then one refill would be enough to drop irrigate the sapling for a few days. Hundreds of thousands of children, students and youths have adopted this method reducing the mortality of saplings in water scarce areas of Gujarat. Hence, every year on World Environment Day, my mantra is 'Sow trees – Sow earthen pots'.

Energy Reforms - Essential For Mitigation

During my initial years of governance in Gujarat, Energy Sector Reforms posed a daunting challenge due to their serious political fallouts, since it would concern millions of farmers in the State, in addition to dealing with strong unions of workers and other vested interests in the gigantic Government Electricity Utility. Even before the Central Government in India enacted the Electricity Act, 2003, in September the same year I got a careful road map prepared suggesting the framework for separation of generation, transmission

219.067 MW Dhuvaran Gas Based Combined Cycle Power Plant

Gujarat State Electricity Corporation Ltd.
District Anand, Gujarat

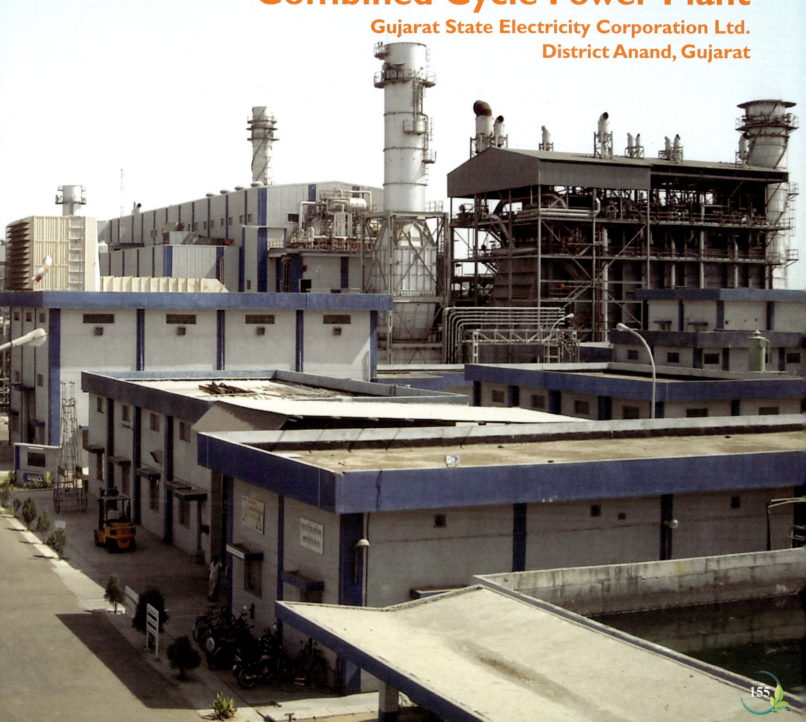

Energy Reforms - Essential For Mitigation

374.571 MW Utran Extension Gas Based Combined Cycle Power Plant

**Gujarat State Electricity Corporation Ltd.
District Surat, Gujarat**

and distribution of electricity in my State to make the power sector more dynamic and sensitive to the needs of changing times. And hence, we enacted Gujarat Electricity Industry (Reorganisation and Regulations) Act in May, 2003. This resulted in unbundling of massive and almost unmanageable Gujarat Electricity Board into several separate companies for generation, transmission and distribution. In those early reform years, while we sufficiently recognised the need to provide uninterrupted power supply to the people and specially to those in rural areas; we also consciously took into account the higher costs in terms of financial resources and the adverse impacts of burning of fossil fuel for the generation of required power due to the emission of greenhouse gases. Therefore, along with taking measures for cost efficiency, I particularly emphasised on efficient use of electrical energy by reducing transmission and distribution losses and encouraging the use of energy efficient equipments.

Energy Reforms - Essential For Mitigation

Improvement in Power Generation Efficiency

The State Power Utilities have been adopting better Operation and Maintenance (O&M) practices to reduce Station Heat Rate, Auxiliary Consumption, etc. The energy audits of power plants have been carried out and by implementation of recommendations given in the energy audit reports, the generating stations have achieved a saving of 13,035.831 MWh of energy per annum. Renovation and Modernisation (R&M) of low performing units in phased manner (Kutch Lignite Thermal Power Station (KLTPS) 1 & 2, Ukai 1 & 2 and Gandhinagar 1 & 2) has been carried out.

Due to the use of washed coal, the energy consumed in transportation, handling and milling has been optimised as the inert material from coal is eliminated. This helps in reducing the auxiliary consumption of equipments involved in coal processing because the use of improved coal ultimately results in reduction of emission of GHG as compared to conventional coal.

For reducing the transmission losses and improving power factor, lines with higher

Gas Based Combined Cycle Power Plant
District Surat, Gujarat

transmission voltages have been laid. More number of high voltage sub stations have been set up and capacitor banks have been installed at various sub stations in the State.

Distribution efficiency measures include installation of Energy Efficient Submersible Pump sets on agricultural locations, installation of Automatic Power Factor Control Panels for improvement in Power Factor and providing Amorphous Transformers by gradually replacing conventional Transformers in the Distribution Network. These activities have cumulatively resulted in substantial energy savings and efficient use of available energy.

The combined efforts of reforms in Generation, Transmission and Distribution Sectors have moderated the requirements of additional generation of electricity using fossil fuel in order to meet the increase in demand of electricity. By improving the overall efficiency of the power plants and improving the performance standards of Transmission and Distribution network lesser emission of the GHG has been achieved.

From 2000-01 to 2007-08, Gujarat's net electricity generation (Million kWh) has increased by 28.75% and the CO_2 intensity (tCO_2/MWh) has reduced by 4.18% vis-a-vis India's net generation, which has increased by 37.34% and CO_2 intensity has reduced only by 0.93%.

Promoted Gas for a Better Tomorrow

GSECL has set up 219 MW Gas Based Combined Cycle Power Plant at Dhuvaran (District Anand). The estimated reduction in CO_2 emission from this project is 214,000 tCO_2 per annum. GSECL has taken up implementation of highly efficient 375 MW Combined Cycle Gas Based Power Plant at Utran (District Surat) on Engineering, Procurement and Construction (EPC) basis.

Fuel Conversion

Gujarat Alkalies and Chemicals Ltd (GACL) 90 MW captive power plant was converted from Naphtha to Gas in 2001 and was registered as a CDM project. Due to this the estimated reduction in CO_2 emission is 99,462 tCO_2 per annum.

Gujarat Industries and Power Corporation Ltd (GIPCL) 140 MW power plant has been switched over from Naphtha to Gas in 2003. As a result of this, the estimated reduction in CO_2 emission is approx. 80,000 tCO_2 per annum.

Others

In view of high Global Warming Potential (GWP) of N_2O gas, State owned Gujarat Narmada Valley Fertilizer Company has put a special catalyst in the ammonia combustion furnace for reducing emission level. The equivalent CO_2 emission reduction will be 332,948 MT CER, taking 310 GWP as a factor for N_2O.

Impact of Transmission and Distribution losses and Generation Efficiency

The Transmission and Distribution (T&D) loss during the year 2000-01 was 35.27% and the generation efficiency, i.e. Plant Load Factor (PLF) was 67.85%. The installed capacity was 8,588 MW at the end of 2000-2001, which was increased to 9,864 MW at the end of 2008-09. The power demand was 7,289 MW and 9,437 MW in corresponding years. During 2001 to 2009, the T&D losses were reduced by 14.13% and the generation efficiency was increased by 7.47%, which was equivalent to capacity addition of around 1,276 MW – equivalent to 59.31% of the additional generation demand of 2,148 MW. Thus, the total increase in power demand is 29.47%, while the actual capacity addition is only 14.85%, resulting into an impact of 14.62%. The year-wise details of installed capacity, demand catered to, T&D losses, etc., are tabulated below:

Year	Installed capacity in MW	% PLF	Maximum Demand catered to in MW	Energy Generated million kWh	% T&D Losses
2000-01	8,588	67.85	7,289	41,983	35.27
2001-02	8,657	67.14	7,064	44,020	34.20
2002-03	8,582	69.69	7,743	46,794	35.90
2003-04	8,689	64.72	7,605	46,123	30.90
2004-05	8,761	70.13	8,078	49,437	30.64
2005-06	8,977	68.01	8,170	52,232	26.51
2006-07	9,561	67.53	8,538	53,520	22.20
2007-08	9,942	76.19	9,335	58,825	21.80
2008-09	9,864	75.32	9,437	60,826	21.14

Source: Energy and Petrochemicals Department, 2010

Gas (Cleaner Fuel) Based Power Stations Installed In The State

Existing Gas Based Power Stations in Gujarat

Station's Name	Capacity in MW
Utran Gas Based	135
Utran Gas Based Expansion	375
Dhuvaran Gas Based - Stage-I	107
Dhuvaran Gas Based - Stage-II	112
Gujarat State Electricity Generation Ltd., Hazira	156
Gujarat Industries Power Company Limited - GPS Stage-I	145
Gujarat Industries Power Company Limited - GPS Stage-II	165
Gujarat Paguthan Energy Company Limited-GPS	655
ESSAR	515
A. E. Co.	100
SUGEN – Combined Cycle Power Plant	1,147
GANDHAR – Gas Based Power Station	657
KAWAS – Gas Based Power Station	656
Total	**4,925**

Gas Based Power Stations under implementation in Gujarat

Station's Name	Capacity in MW
Gujarat State Electricity Generation Limited	360
Dhuvaran Combined Cycle Power Plant	360
GSPC Pipavav Power Company Limited	700
Total	**1,420**

Source: Energy and Petrochemicals Department, 2010

Energy Efficiency in State Capital

It is a fact that comfortable standard of living and quality of human life has become increasingly dependent on energy. The only way to cope up with such growing dependence is adoption of energy conservation measures in every possible way. What better example to spread this message across the State could be than to adopt such measures in the capital city of Gandhinagar within the Government's Secretariat Complex housing all the Ministries and State Government offices. The fact that total power demand of Government buildings in the capital city was 10 MW with an annual electricity bill of ₹ 150 million*, prompted me to begin this campaign from the Secretariat Complex. This complex comprising of a four-storied Legislative Assembly Building, ten blocks of ten-storied buildings and four blocks each of three-storied buildings, had an annual electricity consumption of 7.87 million kWh in the year 2001-2002, costing about ₹ 35.38 million*.

*1 US$ ≅ ₹ 47

Details of Electrical Installations in Secretariat Complex, Gandhinagar, Gujarat

Electrical Utility	Numbers/Capacity
1,000 kVA Transformers	8
Pumps for Water Supply	2 (41 HP), 4 (25 HP)
Central Air-conditioning (A.C.) Plant	1,050 Tonnes
1.5 Tonne Window/Split Air-conditioner	500
150 litres Water Coolers	125
Lifts (Elevators) 2.5 m/s, 1.5 m/s, 1 m/s	46
Escalators	4
Ceiling Fans	12,000
Tubelight Fittings	27,000
Computers	3,000 (now increased to 8,500)
Light Poles in compound	210
Halogen Fittings in Assembly Hall	48 (1,000 watt each)

Source: Roads and Buildings Department, 2009

Energy Reforms - Essential For Mitigation

For the contract demand of 3,400 kVA, 11 kV electrical supply has been arranged from Torrent Power A.E. Co. Ltd., Ahmedabad.

The following energy conservation measures were adopted with an additional investment of ₹ 13.8 million* in stages. These resulted in total savings of 6.103 million kWh from July 2002 to June 2009:

- Replacing 17,500 conventional tubelights with T/5 tubelights to reduce electricity consumption by 44%.
- Application of Sustained Red Green & Blue Light (SRGB) fittings by replacing 1,000 watts Halogen fittings in Assembly Hall to reduce electricity consumption by 67% (illumination level increased from 350 to 550 lumens).

Sardar Vallabhbhai Patel Bhavan
Gandhinagar, Gujarat

- Replacing conventional Light fittings in the campus with Metal Helide fittings to reduce consumption by 40%.
- Replacement of conventional Cooling Tower by FRP Cooling Tower (1,500 TR) to reduce consumption by 210 HP.
- Staggering the timings of the lifts - considering the office timings of 10.30 to 18.10 hrs, in each Block 2 lifts to be operated only in rush hours, i.e. 10.00 to 11.00, 14.00 to 15.00 and 17.30 to 18.30 hrs, for the remaining time period only 1 lift to be operative.
- Replacement of 130 window type AC machines by new ones to increase efficiency.
- Staggering the timings of AC Plants.
- Monitoring the Transformer load – stopping three 1,000 kVA Transformers for at least three months in winter.

Growth Of Gas Based Power Stations

Year	India / Gujarat	Total Installed capacity (MW)	Gas Installed Capacity (MW)	% of Total Installed Capacity	% increase compared to 2003
2003	India	107,877	11,633	10.78	--
	Gujarat	8,606	1,967	22.86	--
2008	India	143,061	14,877	10.40	27.89
	Gujarat (Existing)	9,841	2,294	23.31	16.62
2012	India	221,761	21,720	9.79	86.71
	Gujarat	18,764	6,346	33.82	222.60
(Expected by end of 11th Five Year Plan)					

*1 US$ ≅ ₹ 47

Source: Energy and Petrochemicals Department, 2009

Energy Reforms - Essential For Mitigation

Application Of T/5 Tubelights By Replacement Of Conventional Tubelights
Gandhinagar, Gujarat

These measures not only proved to be helpful in reducing energy consumption, but also helped in maintaining the maximum demand constant, despite an additional 800 kW load during this period. Thus, an additional saving of ₹ 7.20 million* was achieved in terms of probable increase in fixed charges, which otherwise would have become necessary due to an increase in load of 800 kW.

A similar example is that of the street lights in the capital city of Gandhinagar. Replacement of 7,500 conventional lamps of 100 watt each with 14 watt T/5 tubes has resulted in yearly savings of 2.35 million kWh of electricity with a financial saving of ₹ 7.65 million* per year. Having implemented

*1 US$ ≅ ₹ 47

Replacement Of Conventional Cooling Tower By FRP Cooling Tower (1500 TR)
Gandhinagar, Gujarat

this in the year 2004-05, the total energy saving realised on account of these measures alone is 8.56 million kWh, which is worth ₹ 20.30 million*.

Installation of load managers in the Main Road Switching Points, microprocessor based easy ON/OFF system for street lights (based on actual Sunrise and Sunset pattern), total Dim Down system, phase wise Dim Down system, continuous filtered power and GSM based connectivity for effective monitoring of switching points are some of the measures that are planned to be implemented in near future in order to save energy even amidst a demand scenario which is ever increasing.

*1 US$ ≅ ₹ 47

Wind Energy

Gujarat is blessed with around 1,600 km of coastline, with excellent wind speeds for harnessing wind power especially in the Saurashtra peninsula. The State has also been rated as having the highest wind power potential in the country, i.e. around 9,675 MW.

800 kW Wind Power Generation Project

District Jamnagar, Gujarat

The Sun And The Wind

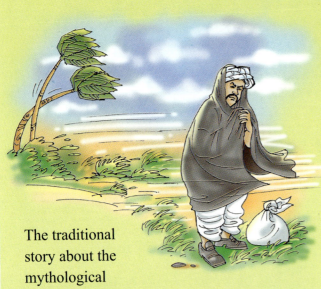

The traditional story about the mythological competition of superiority between Sun and the Wind was narrated to me during my childhood by one of the teachers in primary school. These two great forces of nature squabbled with each other in order to prove their strength and superiority. When the argument failed, they decided to test their strengths by focusing on a lone pedestrian wearing a heavy cloak. The condition was, whoever would cause the traveller to take off his cloak, would be declared the winner and hence stronger.

First blew the Wind and the Sun retired behind a cloud. The harder it blew the tighter the traveller wrapped the cloak round himself and at last the wind had to abandon its effort in utter despair. Then came the Sun shining brightly in the sky and throwing its blaze with full force. After a while, the traveller found it hard to walk due to blistering heat and perspiration. Ultimately, he took off his cloak and put it on his shoulders. The Sun defeated the Wind.

The story had a different moral context – persuasion and kindness have greater and more effective results than severity. These values were inculcated upon my mind in those initial years of school. However, the story also made an everlasting impact on my mind about the Eternal Power of two great forces of nature – the Sun and the Wind.

I have been consistently trying to increase the wind power generation capacity in Gujarat through successive policy frameworks. As a result of this, there has been a phenomenal rise in wind power generation. From 119.495 MW in 2002 it increased to 1,865 MW in 2010. These wind farms have generated 6,978 million kWh of electricity over the last eight years. This has helped emission reduction equivalent to 1.56 million tCO_2.

The Growth Of Wind Power
800 kW Wind Turbine

District Jamnagar, Gujarat

Year-wise Capacity Additions In Wind Energy, Units Generated And Reduction Of CO_2 Emissions

Year	Capacity addition (MW)	Cumulative capacity (MW)	Electricity generation (MkWh)	CO_2 emission reduction (tonnes)
2002-03	6.200	119.495	146.90	32,758.7
2003-04	28.925	148.420	150.45	33,550.4
2004-05	51.525	199.945	201.61	44,959.0
2005-06	84.600	284.545	286.04	63,786.9
2006-07	283.950	568.495	454.95	101,453.9
2007-08	616.355	1,184.850	851.33	189,846.6
2008-09	313.605	1,498.455	2,759.00	615,257.0
2009-10	297.125	1,795.905	2,127.21	474,367.8
2010-11 (up to July)	69.675	1,865.580		
Total			**6,977.49**	**1,555,980.3**

Source: Gujarat Energy Development Agency, 2010

Growth Of Wind Power Generation

Year	India/Gujarat	Total installed capacity (MW)	Wind installed capacity (MW)	% of total installed capacity	% increase in 2008 compared to 2003
2003	India	107,877	1,871	1.73	--
	Gujarat	8606	181	2.10	--
2008	India	143,061	8,698	6.08	364.89
	Gujarat	9,841	1,255	12.75	593.37

Source: Gujarat Energy Development Agency, 2009

In November 2008, Gujarat notched the first prize and won the Best Wind Developer State Award in India for maximum capacity addition in wind power generation for the year 2006-08, with a growth rate of 99.64% during two fiscals – 2006-07 and 2007-08, along the coast of Saurashtra.

In 2009, my Government announced an amendment in the Wind Power Policy to tap around 10,000 MW potential along the coastal areas of the State. Today, this policy has undergone major revisions to attract more investors in the field. The amendments in the Wind Power Policy, 2009 include:

Best Wind Power Developer State Award,
(Percentage Increase - 1st prize),
Wind India 2008,
November 25-26, Chennai

- Renewable energy power purchase obligation increased from the existing 2% to 10%.

- A mechanism was established to facilitate the creation of Renewable Energy Certificates from renewable energy obligation of utilities/open access and captive consumers, using conventional fuel.

- Gujarat Energy Transmission Company (GETCO) will either provide grid connectivity to wind farms or permit private producers for laying transmission lines.

The Eternal Power Of Sun & Wind

The initiative has resulted in MOUs with private investors for setting up 6124 MW Wind Power Plants in the State at the Vibrant Gujarat Global Investors Summit 2009 held in Ahmedabad.

Harnessing Wind Power Potential On Coastline

800 kW Wind Turbine
District Jamnagar, Gujarat

Renewable Energy At Vibrant Gujarat Global Investors Summit 2009

- With the Special Incentive Package announced for Solar and Wind Power Generation Projects, the Renewable Energy Sector received a boost at Vibrant Gujarat Global Investors' Summit (VGGIS) 2009.

- Sector-wise, the highest number of MOUs were signed in the renewable energy sector – 32% – envisaging a total capital investment equivalent to around US$24 billion.

- 66 MOUs were inked for projects based on Solar and Wind energy generation of more than 10,321 MW. (6124 MW in Wind, 1560 MW Solar Thermal, 1837 MW Solar PV, over 700 MW in Bio energy and 5 MW each in Geo-thermal and Wave Power Plants in the State).

- Over the next five years these projects are envisaged to generate employment to over 45,000 people in Gujarat.

Solar Energy

With high solar radiation levels for almost 300 days in a year, Gujarat has vast potential for Solar Power Generation Projects. We have been working on a comprehensive policy to tap and promote solar power as an additional source of energy. We have done so by establishing projects in vast barren tracts of land in backward regions of the State, and thereby contributing to the creation of livelihood for the local people. The salient features and incentives provided under the Solar Power Policy, 2009 of my Government are given in the following pages.

Solar PV Street Lighting System
Anand Sarovar Garden, District Patan, Gujarat

The Eternal Power Of Sun & Wind

Solar Water Heating System (Capacity – 2,500 lpd)
Muni Seva Ashram, District Vadodara, Gujarat

- The policy is to remain in operation upto 31.3.2014. Solar Power Generators (SPG) installed and commissioned during the operative period to become eligible for incentives for a period of 25 years from the date of commissioning or for the life span of SPG whichever is earlier.

- A maximum of 500 MW SPG to be allowed for installation during the policy period.

- The minimum project capacity of a SPG, in case of Solar Photovoltic (SPV) and Solar Thermal (ST) to be 5 MW each.

- Any company or body corporate or association or body of individuals, etc., to be eligible for setting up of such projects either in captive use or for selling electricity.

- Electricity generated from the SPGs to be exempted from payment of electricity duty and also from demand cut to the extent of 50% of installed capacity.

- Purchase price of electricity from Solar Photovoltaic at ₹ 15/kWh and for Solar Thermal at ₹ 11/kWh (much higher than conventional Thermal Energy rates).

- These projects are expected to result in reduction of almost 21 million tCO_2 emission every year.

1 US$ ≅ ₹ 47

Lighting With The Sun : Solar Photovoltaic Systems

In remote tribal areas of Gujarat namely the villages of Kanzal and Dhirkhadi in Narmada District, the sun never sets! There are 202 tribal families in Kanzal which continue working after dusk as do 257 in Dhirkhadi as children complete school homework and women cook in bright smoke free light. Moreover, 35 solar PV streetlights in Kanzal and 105 in Dhirkhadi make sure that the village streetlights are well lit even after the sun has gone down. Similarly, 36 villages in the forests of Junagadh and Porbandar districts have been electrified by the solar PV systems. Water pumps driven by Solar PV energy have also been installed by Gujarat Energy Development Agency (GEDA) for community drinking water facilities in many remote corners of the State. About 700 Solar PV lights illuminate the streets of 3,000 salt pan workers' households in eight coastal districts of Gujarat, where salt production is a major occupation.

The Solar Projects to be established pursuant to this policy, in the State, are expected to generate 20,000 million kWh of electric power annually.

We have also been working with Clinton's Climate Initiative to set up the world's largest Solar Power Project (3,000 MW) in arid regions of Kutch in Gujarat. This would be a landmark wherein all the raw materials including glass and panels will be produced locally to bring about a substantial decrease in the costs. Presently, feasibility of availability and cost of critical factors like solar radiation, labour, land characteristics, seismological data, etc., are being examined.

Gujarat Energy Development Agency (GEDA) Promotes:

- Devices based on Renewable Energy Sources such as Solar Cookers, Solar Water Systems, Solar Stills, Biogas Plants, SPV Street-lights and home-lights, Solar Portable Lanterns, Water Pumping Windmills and Wind Turbines.

- Devices that save energy, such as Improved Crematoria, Natural Water Coolers, Diamond Hot Plate, Mono Block Lathe, CFLs, T-5 tube-lights and electronic accessories (ballasts, chokes, regulators), Improved electronic accessories, Improved Potters' Kiln and Potters' Wheel, Improved Bullock Cart.

- Demand Side Management for Agriculture Pump Sets.

- Energy Audit in public utilities.

- Energy Audit Study of water pumping stations and implementation of recommended measures.

- Energy Audit of designated consumers under the mandate of Government of Gujarat.

- Demonstration of Energy Efficient Street Lighting Systems by Urban Local Bodies.

- Biomass Gasifier based thermal and electrical power generation applications.

- Awareness Workshops and Training Programmes in Colleges, Schools and for Professionals.

Waste - to - Energy Power Generation Project (Capacity - 2 MW)
Kanoria Chemicals, Ankleshwar, District Bharuch, Gujarat

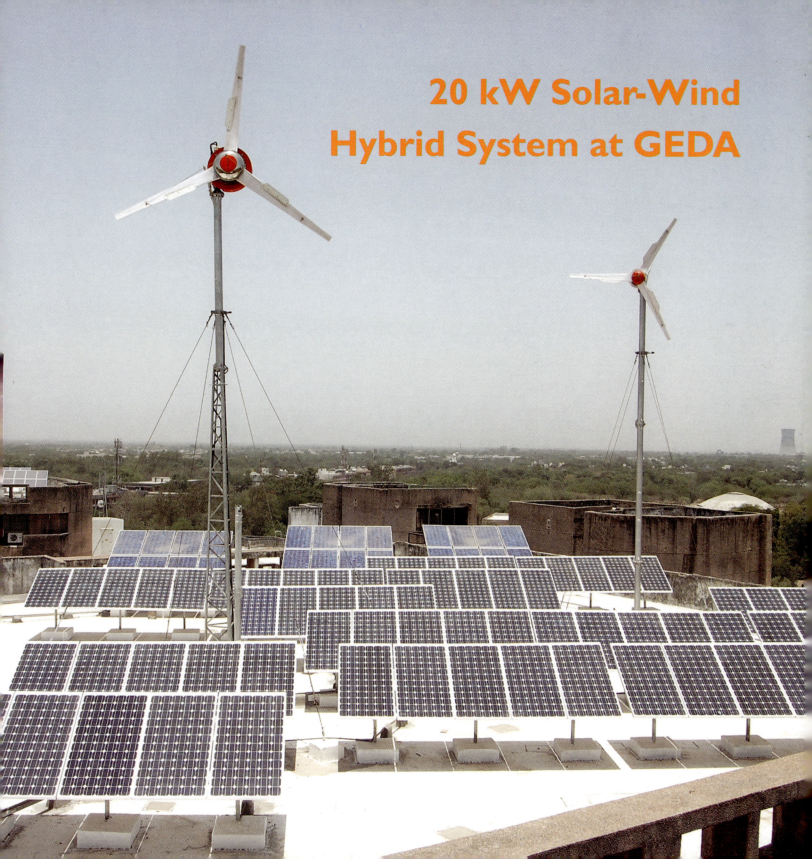

Child Energy Guardians (Bal Urja Rakshak Dal)

I have always believed in the enormous, inherent power of children to facilitate changes in social habits and practices. This inspired me to announce, in 2003, a unique scheme of 'Child Energy Guardians'. The aim was to mobilise children as energy guardians, to motivate responsible, rational and restrained use of energy in their homes, schools and community by encouraging right and honest choices. This pioneering experiment to create an energy-wise Gujarat has significantly resulted in following achievements:

- 'Child Energy Guardian' teams have been established in 3,600 schools (1,800 primary and 1,800 secondary schools).

- 50,000 children have been enrolled and mobilised as Child Energy Guardians.

- Participatory awareness programmes have been conducted in urban, semi-urban, rural and tribal regions of the State with participation of over two million people.

- 1,800 'Energy Pioneers' have been identified and selected from amongst school teachers all over the State, who have undergone extensive training and sufficient hands-on experience as how to conduct energy audit in schools and homes at Science City in Ahmedabad.

- 9,000 home energy audits and 1,800 school energy audits have been conducted by the motivated 'Child Energy Guardians' Force.

- 4 million kWh have been saved per year at a conservative estimate of 1 kWh/hr.

- Edutainment (fun-and-learn) activities, such as puppet shows and other cultural events, have been specially designed and organized for school children to understand the basics of energy concepts, forms and types of energy and energy conservation in homes and schools.

- The programme, as a participatory awareness generation module, has helped to reduce carbon footprints in Gujarat. This is because, one kWh of energy saved is 2.5 kWh of energy generated. The 4 million kWh of electricity saved on a conservative estimate has led to reduction of CO_2 emission to the extent of around one tonne annually.

Coastal Sustainable Livelihoods

Integration of Climate Change adaptation into all aspects of policy formulation and implementation for poverty reduction has been one of the high priority areas for my Government.

Fishing Vessels At Veraval Harbour
District Junagadh, Gujarat

Coastal Sustainable Livelihoods

Aquaculture On Gujarat Coast

I personally feel that Governments should focus more on broad and integrated development strategies to equip the poor and vulnerable people to withstand Climate shocks. Coastal Gujarat, having over 1,600 km exposure to Arabian sea, the longest exposure in India, will be more vulnerable to potential sea level rise, flooding, cyclones and damages to infrastructure.

It also houses a large fishing community. Therefore, in 2007 we devised a new integrated development programme for coastal communities known as 'Sagar Khedu Sarvangi Vikas Yojana' (Multi Dimensional Development Package for Coastal Communities).

Coastal Sustainable Livelihoods

Shrimps Grading At A Plant, Gujarat

12-Points Of "Sagarkhedu Sarvangi Vikas Package" (Multi Dimensional Development Package For Coastal Communities)

1. Skill Upgradation Programmes
2. Creating Employment Opportunities
3. Development through Education
4. Health Services for all
5. Access to Pure Drinking Water
6. Home for all
7. Soil Conservation
8. Water Management
9. Electrification
10. Capacity Building Programmes
11. Development of Salt Pan Workers ("Agarias")
12. National Security

This is a unique convergence model with an allocation of ₹ 110 billion* covering 38 sub-divisions of Gujarat coast and a population of around 6 million. It is for the first time that any Indian State has announced such a programme that addresses the specific problems and needs of people living in coastal areas. The programme goes beyond mere livelihood issues. Recognising the fact that people living in coastal areas play a distinctive role not only in the economy but in the preservation of eco-system, the programme takes a holistic and integrated view to address the needs of their livelihoods, keeping in mind the dignity of life. It proposes specific and time bound action plan for improving wage and self-employment, capacity building and skill upgradation, educational facilities, health infrastructure, drinking water, housing, salinity ingress, electrification and water conservation, development of salt pan workers and national security.

*1 US$ ≅ ₹ 47

Coastal Sustainable Livelihoods

It has a special focus on the upgradation of technology in traditional professions like fishing as well as salt pan work. Strengthening internal security on the coastal line with the use of state-of-the-art technology in modernising 10 Police Stations, equipping the Police with new jeeps, motor cycles, computers and communication network at an expenditure of around ₹ 600 million* in the first phase and development of Police Stations with an outlay of ₹ 2,200 million* in the second phase is also part of the plan.

Each of the 38 sub-divisions will get at least one Industrial Training Institute (ITI). Further, it will have special part time vocational training programmes in 14 trades pertaining to coastal areas. A special training is also proposed for marine technicians and marine engineering courses. Tourism activities would be initiated with a view to immediately increase related employment.

*1 US$ ≅ ₹ 47

Squids Processing At A Plant, Gujarat

On the educational front, 88 new primary and secondary schools and 8 new polytechnics, which would cost approximately ₹ 2,000 million* are being planned. Naval National Cadet Corps courses would be offered in all the coastal educational institutions. The entire coastal belt will be given access to community and primary health centres along with qualitative improvement of the existing ones.

There is a major focus on nutrition of the children and pregnant mothers. Four new Primary Health Centres (PHCs) and 9 mobile health care units are being set up in addition to modernizing of Veraval

Education in Fisheries at Gujarat Coast

General Hospital at a cost of ₹ 125 million*. A part of the plan is to provide drinking water through surface pipelines to each of the 3,000 villages in coastal belt. Around 50 to 60 villages shall be provided drinking water through reverse osmosis process. Around 15,000 houses for poor people and 82,000 toilets will also be provided. A sum of ₹ 350 million* is being allocated for village infrastructure. A major programme of ₹ 2,000 million* is being undertaken for soil conservation to prevent salinity ingress by way of constructing tidal regulators, spreading canals, protection walls, checkdams, recharging of ground water and integrated watershed projects. In addition ₹ 480 million* have been provided for water conservation by way of constructing 600 checkdams and deepening of 600 village ponds. Around

Fisheries Training Programme
Veraval, Gujarat

125,000 km long electricity distribution service line will be renovated with anti-corrosive materials costing ₹ 450 million*. Apart from these 9 transmission sub-stations at a cost of ₹ 340 million* will be established in the coastal sub-divisions. There are about 40 villages where power would be provided with the help of solar energy.

*1 US$ ≅ ₹ 47

Students of Fisheries College
Veraval, Gujarat

Coastal Sustainable Livelihoods

There is a special package for the salt pan workers. This includes provision of clean drinking water, school rooms, medical mobile vans, protective kits, rationing mobile vans, rest sheds and community centres as also free uniform and educational kits for their children. This programme is being implemented with a strong resolve of my Government with the hope of betterment of every individual in coastal areas.

Skill Upgradation In Coastal Belt

Expected Outcomes Of Multi Dimensional Development Package For Coastal Communities

1. Creation of new job avenues will reduce the distress of frequent migration.

2. Upgradation of technical skills through an ITI in each sub-division will help educated youth to find productive employment.

3. Off-season employment for fishermen will be available.

4. Enhanced capacity of fishermen through training and modern equipment will augment fish production and thereby their standard of living.

5. Enhanced export avenues of various value added marine products will also be available.

6. Special package for Salt pan workers will improve the quality of life of salt pan workers at large.

7. Substantial check in salinity ingress would lead to better agricultural productivity and safe drinking water.

8. Adequate availability of basic amenities in rural households Coastal areas will reduce their vulnerability to Climate Shocks.

This is a historic package unparalleled in whole of India.

Disaster Preparedness In Coastal Areas

Gujarat State Disaster Management Authority (GSDMA) has taken many initiatives for disaster preparedness and risk reduction in coastal areas. GSDMA has prepared a comprehensive Hazard Risk and Vulnerability Atlas (HRVA) for the State covering six major hazards namely Earthquake, Tsunami, Flood, Cyclone, Drought and Chemical and Industrial hazards. One of the key objectives behind this is to create communities that are aware of the steps to be taken in a pre, during and post disaster situation to protect lives and property. The programme focuses on awareness generation, education, training, management and recovery at community, district and state levels.

Following initiatives have been taken up under the programme:

- Training of Trainers (TOT) for Cyclone Management and Flood Rescue have been organized in collaboration with Municipal Fire Departments and local NGOs.

- Hazard manuals for cyclone, earthquake, flood and industrial accidents have been developed and distributed to all the districts.

- In addition, leaflets and do's and don'ts along with safety tips for addressing cyclone, floods, earthquakes and other hazards have been developed and distributed during training programmes to all the district officials for further dissemination.

- Standard Operating Procedures (SOPs) and manuals for first aid, search and rescue and first aid pocket size booklets and handbooks have been distributed to different Disaster Management Teams.

- Gujarat Institute of Disaster Management (GIDM) also organises regular training programmes for district and grass root level officials, on cyclone and flood preparedness especially during the pre-monsoon season starting from May to July.

'Green' (Golden Jubilee) Pledge

I have believed in the power of people's participation to bring extraordinary results in any developmental effort. However, before physical participation, on a more metaphysical and spiritual plane, people have to mentally adopt and assimilate a thought, identify and integrate that with their inner and spiritual energies and then redirect their efforts into achieving and realising it.

Pledges From Inside

'Green' (Golden Jubilee) Pledge
Narendra Modi Administering A Green Pledge

This will ensure willing participation and the results are quick and long lasting. At the same time, people feel a sense of pride in contributing their mite to something that the Government of the day may have initiated. This was my motivation behind 'The Golden Jubilee Pledge Enlightenment Chariot'.

'Green' (Golden Jubilee) Pledge

Women (Power) Pledges

The State of Gujarat, after coming into being as a separate Indian State on 1st May, 1960 (based on linguistic reorganisation of States in the country); has been seen to be a role model of all round and inclusive development in the country. Therefore, we should approach our golden jubilee of formation in the year 2010 not only with a sense of celebration for achievements of the past but with also a pledge, taken deep within, by every citizen of the State, to contribute and make Gujarat an even better Gujarat, a more prosperous Gujarat, a healthier Gujarat, a Greener and Cleaner Gujarat, and a more Modern Gujarat.

'Green' (Golden Jubilee) Pledge

The methodology adopted here is that of a symbolic chariot moving into every village and town in the State, making people take individual and collective pledges touching a wide variety of subjects like conservation of environment and judicious use of natural resources, education, social service, civic habits, etc. The chariot moves daily, from place to place, people gather and take pledges individually and collectively and a sense of camaraderie, pride and responsibility builds up for participation in the development of the State.

'Green' (Golden Jubilee) Pledge

Young Pledges

So far 3,378,911 people have taken individual pledges out of 7,707,457 who attended the chariot celebrations. An encouraging number indeed.

Students from 9,133 schools and colleges have participated in this. And more importantly 1,028,391 trees have been planted in the process. Many of these pledges would help people in my State to prepare for Climate Change adaptation. I call it 'Adaptation the pure Democratic way'.

Power Of Pledges For Adaptation

- I will plant and nurture at least ten trees.

- I will celebrate my kid's birthday by getting a tree planted.

- I will use water and electricity judiciously.

- I will judiciously use water for irrigation.

- I will provide mechanism for rain water harvesting in my building.

- I will protect myself and make people aware about the need to protect natural resources and national property.

- I will use eco-friendly products.

- I will collect garbage in dust bin only and will not throw litter anywhere.

- I will work sincerely to have more and more villages developed as model villages in my region.

- I will keep my classroom neat and clean.

Capacity building is an explicit part of my strategy to deal with challenges of Climate Change. Developing adequate and appropriate skills amongst critical constituencies of stakeholders, both in public and private sectors and at various levels – regional to local, is as important as developing new technologies and tools for mitigation efforts. Government (the public sector, administrators from civil service, policy planners, regulators and other representative officials), Private sector (industry, users of goods and services); and Academia, NGOs and media are all being targetted by us for capacity building exercise.

Capacity Building

Narendra Modi At TERI, New Delhi

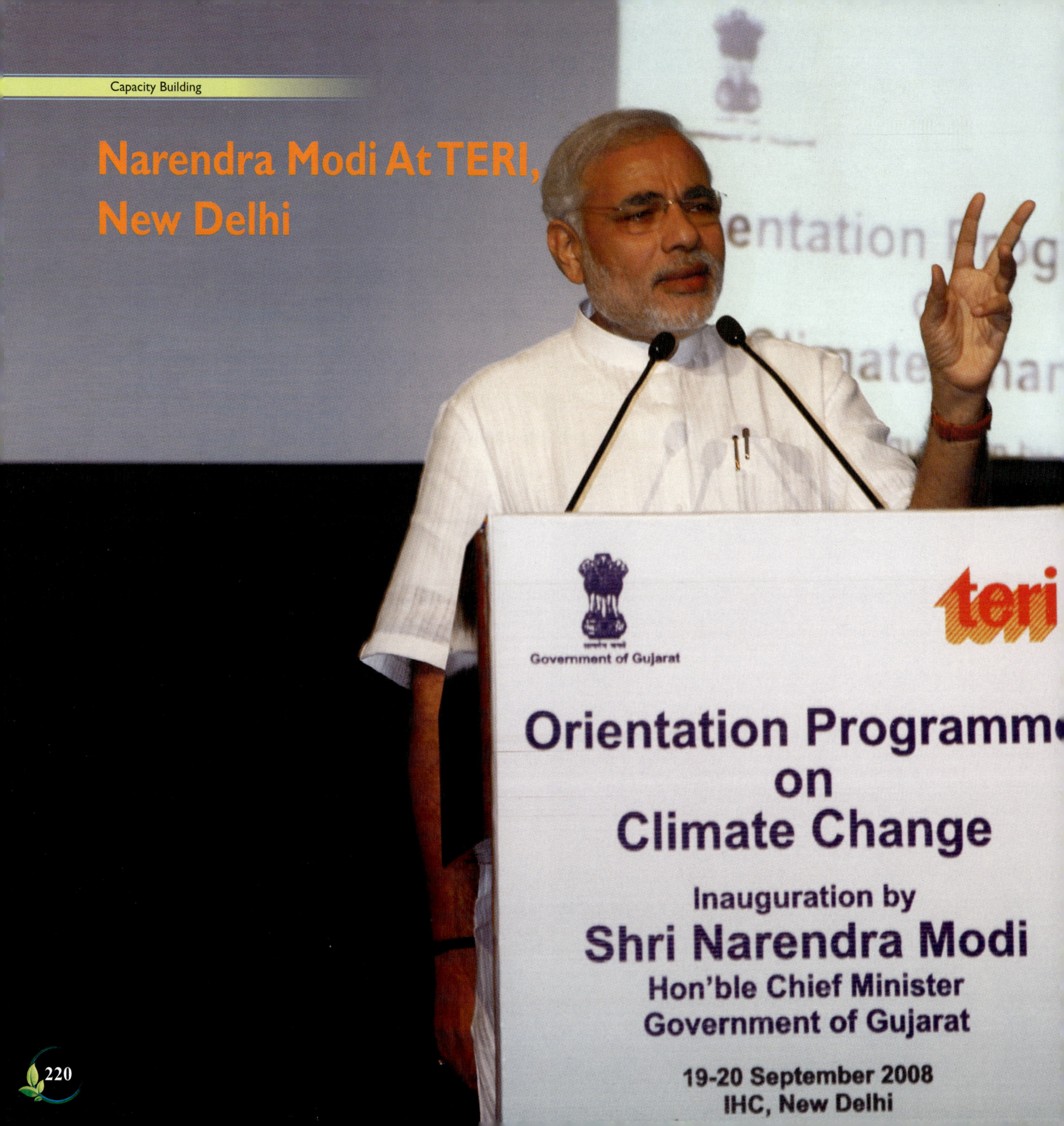

Orientation Programme on Climate Change

Inauguration by
Shri Narendra Modi
Hon'ble Chief Minister
Government of Gujarat

19-20 September 2008
IHC, New Delhi

My effort is to take help of all available expertise within the country and also to network with international organisations. Strategic collaboration with The Energy and Resources Institute (TERI), under the overall supervision of Dr. R.K. Pachauri, Director General, TERI & Chairman, Intergovernmental Panel on Climate Change (IPCC) has resulted in 'Orientation Programmes on Climate Change' for senior Ministers and Civil Servants. The objective has been to train them to integrate Climate Change adaptation and mitigation strategies at all levels of planning and implementation. This exercise has been taken up for the first time by a State Government in the country.

Partnership With The Energy And Resources Institute (TERI)

In September 2008, TERI, headed by IPCC Chairman Dr. R. K. Pachauri executed a Memorandum of Understanding with the Government of Gujarat (GoG) for helping the latter to build capacities for developing Climate Change adaptation and mitigation strategies. It encompasses wide ranging issues from joint mission on National Action Plan on Climate Change and need based orientation programme for officers and policy planners of Government of Gujarat to developing educational curricula, training of teachers and master trainers on Climate Change and related issues. TERI will also facilitate the GoG in building in-house administrative capacity and institutional set up in order to evolve and formulate comprehensive and overarching state-level Climate Change policy cutting across all sustainable development sectors.

We have also established Management Education Centre on Climate Change (MECCC) in the biggest university of the State - The Gujarat University, Ahmedabad. It will focus on capacity building through short term courses (certificate, customised courses, etc.) and long term courses (Post Graduate Diploma), research and development, seminars and symposia, etc. While formal and other educational and capacity building interventions will be the mainstay, projects that demonstrate the feasibility of appropriate solutions to problems will also be carried out.

Gujarat University
Ahmedabad, Gujarat

Management Education Centre On Climate Change (MECCC)

The MECCC aims to impart knowledge on Climate Change and technical and social skills to facilitate appropriate mitigation and adaptation action that deals with issues in conjunction with the larger developmental agenda of our country. This includes changes in curricula at college levels, introduction of various programs at university level and training of professionals and executives in relevant fields. The main objectives of the MECCC courses are to:

- Impart a comprehensive understanding of the natural and artificially induced factors responsible for Climate Change.

- Build capacities to respond appropriately to Climate Change by using tools and techniques for assessing changes and implement mitigation and adaptation measures.

- Help select, design and apply a range of complementary, cohesive tools and concepts as part of a strategic approach to sustainability.

- Enhance communication capabilities to inform and empower through knowledge of organisational and personal learning skills, improved presentation, facilitation and delivery.

Creation of appropriate and dedicated institutional mechanism within my Government to coordinate adaptation planning in diverse sectors has also been a priority area for me. My Government has been a pioneer in whole of India (and even in Asia) to establish a separate Department of Climate Change. Very few nations in the world like Denmark, Australia, New Zealand, United Kingdom, etc., have done this. Following mandates have been entrusted to this new department which I am looking after:

- Preparation of comprehensive multi-dimensional Climate Change Policy for Gujarat State.

- Coordination with all other departments with respect to Climate Change.

- The department would undertake detailed and extensive research and survey with regard to impacts of Climate Change on coastal area. This would cover the possible impacts on Gujarat coast due to sea level rise, changes in agricultural productivity, new challenges to health and infrastructural facilities in the coastal areas and the measures that would be required to deal with them.

- The department would prepare a pro-active policy to convert the challenges of Climate Change into an opportunity. Maximum usage of Green Technology and investments thereof would be promoted. This department would become a nodal agency for turning Green Technology into a new economic driver by creation of extensive employment opportunities.

- Revolving Fund for R&D in Green Technology and promotion of its usage would also be established.

- Intensive efforts will be undertaken for earning maximum Carbon Credits.

- Educational curricula on Climate Change will be prepared and introduced.

- For reducing GHG emission in industries like Cement, Alkalis, Chemical Fertilizers, Textiles and

Capacity Building

Chemicals, etc. new technologies will be developed, along with creation of appropriate regulatory and financial mechanisms.

- Public Participation and Public Awareness will be developed in this cause in an extensive way.

- Cooperation with national and international agencies will be undertaken. Constant interactions and consultation will be undertaken with National Clean Development Authority and the concerned international agencies under the umbrella of United Nations.

I sincerely hope that these efforts at enhancing the skills and strengthening capacities for risk assessment and resilience planning will ultimately result in far reaching impacts on our adaptation and mitigation strategies.

Narendra Modi Being Presented Solar Lantern By Dr. R. K. Pachauri

Conclusion

I have chosen not to get involved in any figures, targets or quantities of emission cuts before embarking on a low carbon growth pathway for Gujarat. My objective has been an integrated strategy of development which makes sufficient allowance for global warming concerns. And after eight years of practical experiences, results seem to justify the development route we have adopted.

My deep conviction in the complementary and supplementary relationship between man and nature has been a renewable resource steering my mind to fight Climate Change. Dealing with Climate Change and protecting the earth for present and future generations is definitely a moral issue both justified in terms of universalistic moral ethics and also what Aristotle termed as 'Situational Ethics'. It is so because the urgency of the situation or, even what has been termed as 'planetary emergency' dictates ubiquitous adoption of this moral, if we use the famous Greek philosopher's framework.

Climate discussions and deliberations have become an integral part of the international fora whether it be G8 meeting, Davos Economic Forum or any other gathering of developed and developing countries. It is disheartening to note that no overall consensus is emerging for reduction in emission with reference to 2°C increase in global temperatures from pre-industrial levels. Copenhagen, December 2009, despite all pomp and show, failed to become 'Hopenhagen' as far as binding solutions beyond Kyoto Protocol were concerned. Now we are talking of actions beyond Copenhagen. Given the constraints of politics and backstage lobbying of vested interests, the internationally binding outcomes may get delayed or may not even be as per exigency of the situation. But time is running out and with each passing month, year and decade the ecological debt of future generation is mounting higher and higher. In such a complex and fluid situation regional and state leaders in democracies (specially federal ones) have a very significant role to play. From creating water and food security, sustainable coastal livelihoods to reducing emissions in transport, industry and creating an overall Climate Change consciousness amongst children, students and other stakeholders; no electoral constraints or any other factors could inhibit our firm devotion to this cause. In fact, Gujarat model could well serve as an example to decision makers across all political spectrums.

Finance and technology are in abundance all over the world. Recent financial crisis and huge recovery packages by all major nations have proved this fact. What is still lacking is strong political will to fight Climate Change and leave the globe still a habitable place for the future generations. I sincerely hope that this compilation of our diverse actions on Climate Change adaptation and mitigation would be a humble reminder to the world community of politicians, both in developing and developed worlds, that the divide between political cycle and carbon cycle can be filled by firm determination and resolute will. This might even set tone for collective action worldwide, even in absence of formal multilateral frameworks.

In retrospect, I feel satisfied that we have woven an appreciable safety net of adaptations by integrated policy frameworks. Our conscious adaptation, planning and creation of Climate defence infrastructure has resulted in increased resilience of rural and vulnerable communities in Gujarat against Climate shocks in the form of droughts, drinking water scarcity, excessive rains and flooding, etc. Transformational changes in my Government's practices and programmes have been felt and experienced at the grassroots and communities have willingly participated to increase their scope and coverage.

Whereas adaptation has a human angle and is more in the form of damage control exercise, mitigation has to be an essential component of a comprehensive Climate Change strategy. It should be clear from the various projects and efforts enumerated in the preceding pages that we have kept constant emphasis on mitigation initiatives. The fact that these efforts need to be supported by national policies, regulations and institutional back up and also by multilateral international consensus which are yet to take definite shape, however, cannot be denied. But undeterred, I have chosen to act on my own within the available means and resources and limited legal frameworks nationally.

For readers of this book my advice is to pause for a moment and think about all that we take from nature in a day to live and then to realise that it does not ask for anything in return. That is what is known as true giving. Then let us not be too selfish to exploit nature mindlessly when the very foundations of our civilisation rest on the harmonious co-existence with nature. Those in Gujarat are part of our multidimensional effort to combat Climate Change but those in other parts of India and rest of the world are most welcome to witness and experience it.

I am aware that a lot more is still to be done in terms of developing special carbon budgeting for growing individual cities, changing urban lifestyles, developing special climate models for coastal Gujarat and generating Climate Change consciousness amongst over 55 million people of my State. For this, we would welcome any help, technical and financial cooperation and offers of handholding from international organisations, national and regional governments and the scientific community world over.

Abbreviation

AMTS	Ahmedabad Municipal Transport Service
AV	Atharva Veda
AWS	Agriculture Weather Station
BOD	Bio Oxygen Demand
BRTS	Bus Rapid Transit System
C	Centigrade
CDM	Clean Development Mechanism
CEPT	Centre for Environmental Planning and Technology
CER	Certified Emission Reduction
CHPH	Canal Head Power House
CNG	Compressed Natural Gas
CO	Carbon Monoxide
CO$_2$	Carbon Dioxide
COD	Chemical Oxygen Demand
CPCB	Central Pollution Control Board
DRMP	Disaster Risk Management Programme
EA	Triennium
EPC	Engineering, Production & Construction
FOB	Fly Over Bridge
FRP	Fibreglass Reinforced Plastic
GACL	Gujarat Alkalies & Chemicals Ltd.
GEDA	Gujarat Energy Development Agency
GERMI	Gujarat Energy Research & Management Institute
GETCO	Gujarat Energy Transmission Company
GHG	Green House Gas
GIDM	Gujarat Institute of Disaster Management
GIPCL	Gujarat Industries & Power Corporation Ltd.
GoG	Government of Gujarat
GoI	Government of India
GSDMA	Gujarat State Disaster Management Authority
GSECL	Gujarat State Electricity Corporation Limited
GSPC	Gujarat State Petroleum Corporation
GUVNL	Gujarat Urja Vikas Nigam Limited

GWP	Global Warming Potential
H₂S	Hydrogen Sulphide
ha	Hectare
HC	Hydro Carbon
HP	Horse Power
HPGP	High Pressure Gas Pipeline
HR	Head Regulator
IIT	Indian Institute of Technology
IPCC	Intergovernmental Panel on Climate Change
ISA	Implementation Support Agencies
ISRO	Indian Space Research Organization
ITI	Industrial Training Institute
kg	Kilogram
KLTPS	Kutch Lignite Thermal Power Station
km	Kilometre
km²	Square Kilometre
KV	Kilovolt
kVA	Kilovolt Ampere
kW	Kilo Watt
kWh	Kilo Watt Hour (unit)
lpd	Litres per day
LPG	Liquefied Petroleum Gas
m	Metre
m²	Square Metre
m³	Cubic Metre
MAF	Million Acre Feet
Mcft	Million Cubic Feet
MCM	Million Cubic Metre
MECCC	Management Education Centre on Climate Change
mg	Milligram
MkWh	Million Kilo Watt Hour
MLD	Million Litres per Day
MMSCMD	Million Metric Standard Cubic Metre Per Day
MOU	Memorandum of Understanding
MT	Metric Tonne
MU	Million Units
MW	Megawatts
MWh	Mega Watt Hour

N_2O	Nitrogen Oxide
NCRMP	National Cyclone Risk Mitigation Project
NGO	Non Governmental Organization
NOx	Nitrogen Oxide
O&M	Operation and Maintenance
PDPU	Pandit Deendayal Petroleum University
pH	Potential of Hydrogen
PHCs	Primary Health Centres
PLF	Plant Load Factor
R&D	Research & Development
R&M	Renovation & Modernization
RBPH	River Bed Power House
₹ (Rs.)	Indian Rupees
RSPM	Respirable Suspended Particulate Matter
SAC	Space Application Center
SGPP	Sewage Gas based Power Plant
SMC	Surat Municipal Corporation
SO_2	Sulphur Dioxide
SOPs	Standard Operating Procedures
Sox	Sulphur Oxide
SPG	Solar Power Generators
SPM	Suspended Particulate Matter
SPPWCP	Sardar Patel Participatory Water Conservation Project
SPV	Solar Photovoltaic
SRFDCL	Sabarmati River Front Development Corporation Ltd.
SRGP	Sustained Red Green & Blue Light
SSP	Sardar Sarovar Project
ST	Solar Thermal
STP	Sewage Treatment Plant
T&D	Transmission and Distribution
TA	Triennium
tCO_2	Tonne Carbon Dioxide
TERI	The Energy and Resources Institute
TOT	Training of Trainers
UNDP	United Nations Development Programme
VGGIS	Vibrant Gujarat Global Investors' Summit
VWS	Village Water and Sanitation Committee
WASMO	Water & Sanitation Management Organisation
WPG	Wind Power Generation